D1271756

THE BUILT,
THE UNBUILT
AND THE UNBUILDABLE

Robert Harbison

THE BUILT,
THE UNBUILT
AND THE UNBUILDABLE

In Pursuit of Architectural Meaning

The MIT Press
Cambridge, Massachusetts

Designed by Liz Rudderham

First MIT Press edition 1991

Printed and bound in Singapore by CS Graphics

Library of Congress Cataloging-in-Publication Data

Harbison, Robert.
        The built, the unbuilt, and the unbuildable : in pursuit of
architectural meaning   /   Robert Harbison.—1st MIT Press ed.
                p.   cm.
        Includes bibliographical references and index.
        ISBN 0–262–08204–7
        1. Architecture—Philosophy.   2. Signs and symbols in
architecture.   3. Architecture and history.   I. Title.
NA2500.H37   1991
720'.1—dc20
                                                                90–27233
                                                                CIP

Contents

For Randy and in memory of Kathy

Preface

THIS BOOK argues that the solidest architectural facts are fictional to a degree. Like much art, buildings often have a virtual or imaginary component, not that they are liable to vanish like thoughts, but that they are more precarious than they ordinarily appear, because preoccupied with meaning something. If stones are not, meanings are perishable and mistakable, local to cultures which fade or undergo convulsive change.

Paintings are less usable than structures, but this circumscribed use is more secure. And yet they too aren't entirely safe from reemployment: most important European religious paintings have been secularized even if not actually cut to new shapes or moved into hostile un-numinous environments. Buildings are defaced by new uses and by disuse; their failure to mean any longer what they did at first can be extraordinarily painful.

Some architects have been more preoccupied than others with such problems, the ways in which the needs that call buildings into existence can limit their form and trap them before long in obsolescence. And so there are a few venerable ways round these limitations on architects' power as artists, and on the inviolability of their products.

This book explores some of the witting and unwitting means by which buildings evade functional necessities, or surpass them even while satisfying them. It is a Romantic approach to this practical art. At any historical moment you chose, the majority of practitioners would rise in irritation or fury against such depiction of their craft. There are a number of reasons why this should be so. First of all, until recently no client would have ventured anywhere near an architect whose work was openly devoted to personal expression. Then, most buildings aren't really architecture. And most important, like thinking about one's feet when one is walking, or one's words when one is talking, self consciousness about one's artistic means prevents the activity from taking place in the normal way, and makes the practitioner like the reconstructor of a lost language.

This supposed war between art and use is really a diversion, however. In what follows I have concentrated on paradoxes and ironies of function, not because I am impatient with the idea of anything working properly, but because these 'malfunctions' form an important part of the story of human purposefulness, designing things for certain jobs, and also changing its mind about how life should be lived and what devices one needs in order to do that best.

Without stretching the truth very far, I think one can say that gardens, monuments, and ruins, those most imaginary and uncompelled categories of building, are machines too, which perform essential services and are by now irreplaceably part of the equipment of life. There are some things one can't imagine life without, and one can very easily imagine life without these three. Yet when one looks for cultures which have foregone any of them, one is driven surprisingly far afield. Still, a lover of these things is tempted to make outrageous and therefore probably embattled claims for them: in spite of all appearance they are the most useful things in the world, to our psychic health. Or, uselessness is the most sublime of all human constructs, and art fulfills itself in floating miles above every desperate human involvement.

I have chosen to see architecture almost wholly through the extremest instances I could find, those which violate ordinary logic and ordinary need, from a belief that the edges of a field are the best guide to the centre, and from a deep liking for exceptions, for unplaceable or unique cases. Obeying a similar prompting I have often loosened the boundary of a category. Thus the reader will sometimes find themes or topics treated metaphorically – a consideration of forts leads on to imitations of fort-features in churches or prisons, and to the variations on fortified forms in Elizabethan prodigy houses. Likewise, the highest flights of city planning carry me onward to fantastic mocked up worlds, created in the service of architecture, national history, or childish fun – Portmeirion, Williamsburg, Disneyland. We detect a similar conceiving impulse, imposing new forms on the world, in some unexpected places. It is a guiding principle here that naiveté (in the maker or the perceiver of buildings) will occasionally stumble on truths hidden from more expert eyes.

It all begins with gardens, the most trusting and innocent of human constructions. Yet, inspecting them, the *supposed* innocence of gardens, one is tempted to call it, for they are places where the undeclared war between architecture and its antitype, nature, between growth and the ordering impulse, is presented as a delicious harmony. They are places which flirt with allowing art to disappear, which seem to embrace principles hostile to form of any kind – irregularity, change, an urge to destroy. This is the hubris of gardens, to think that they could really improve on or collect the unruliness of natural forces and make a scene of it, like a play in which the actors were all wild animals.

The history of man's efforts to fashion art from non-human life is then widened to include a few attempts to give buildings the qualities of creatures, in organic architecture of the English Arts and Crafts and the Catalan eccentric Gaudi. Paradoxical as it sounds in bald statement, the urge to reassimilate architecture to biological forms which precede our own is widely at work, and is only one instance among many of art as a means of reaching primitive stages in the history of the race or the individual, which will necessarily be hypothetical to a high degree.

Monuments are either the nearest or the furthest thing from gardens, furthest in their fixity and permanence, nearest in their gratuitous and self-willed character. Often they are the only stable anchorage in the green sea of a garden, which the giddy traveller clings to in hopes of extracting a firm significance from his unfocused amble among the trees.

How sure of themselves yet how entirely fictional most monuments are. If one inspects the memorials of Washington, for instance, what contradictory messages one receives. The *desire* to symbolize something towers over the specific content, yet small incongruities collect and make their commentary on the blankness, tallness and monotony preached in such enclaves.

The two poles of a monument are the personal and the impersonal, a confiding saint's or great man's cell – the relic monger's haunt – against a battlefield memorial, biting its tongue, imposing silence. Even among anti-monuments one can set the garrulous Oldenburg against the mute Christo. One of the latest monuments brings the two ends of the scale somehow in touch. The Vietnam Memorial in Washington is all words not images, embarrassed not assertive, using no rhetoric hollow or otherwise, yet speaking exhaustively. It forms the universal utterance these structures usually seek without finding.

They are sometimes *silly* heights, but monuments inhabit pinnacles of symbolizing energy from which one can only *descend* to other topics and other types of construction. Fortification can be seen as the maximum of monumental masonry with the minimum of symbolic content, a practical preventive device on which the monument is the post-operative commentary. Yet surviving fortifications (even half surviving ones) have by now become monstrous monuments prompting armies of tourists to assault them.

9

The history of fortification is full of artists commandeered to design them and reversion to more primitive forms under the influence of advances in weaponry. And for several centuries now, forms borrowed from military structures have found non-military, symbolic uses in churches, prisons, private houses, and the municipal buildings of the Fascist era.

There is also some justification for tracing the roots of the largest urban projects, ideal cities of the Renaissance and since, to military purposes. Palmanova, Pienza, Richelieu, Chaux – the interesting survivors are all incomplete or too big, unfilled at the edge or hollow at the core, celibates among cities.

From nightmares of planning and sterile hypothesis to unplanned decay and art returning to the earth it came out of, or, the death of architecture: ruins. However loosely, up till now we have dealt in discernible building types. Ruins on the contrary are not a type but a condition, to single out which would seem as whimsical to some observers as if one collected green buildings or pointed ones. Of course from one perspective ruin is even more accidental than that – ruins are just *in need of repair*, or when things get bad enough, of demolition. Except that for a couple of centuries we have not been able to see it as simply as that.

In fact the question of ruin is an embarrassing litmus test of the view of architecture at work in this book, because ruins are such a glaring example of architecture existing largely in the mind, or in the eye of the beholder. In remote unpopulated places ruins raise no problems, only vastly differing responses. By the Scottish loch, on the Welsh hill, one can say they are just a way of seeing or a state of soul.

But one enters cities, and has more difficulty arguing that large stretches of usable land should be turned over to nothing but *reminders*, stimuli to the historical imagination. A suspicion of crankiness hangs over the ruin-lover, like the monks who built themselves ruined cells in eighteenth-century Rome, or John Soane modelling his London house on ruins not buildings, which is to say on buildings which have failed. The justification is that our history *has* taken that course, and decay is part of life. The most sublime landscapes – mountain ranges – are worlds in slow disintegration. Geology provides parallels to many human methods of immuring or re-using old bits in new structures. The past fertilizes the present, or cascading violently onto it, exerts an immobilizing curse.

In a way the great modern test-case is industrial obsolescence. Piranesi in the present would be most excited by abandoned docks, factories, and mills. There we act out scenarios of work and power, which are satisfied better by the high tech buildings of Richard Rogers, like revived superstition, than by functioning industrial plants, whose wheezing and stamping isn't as picturesque in fact, as when filtered by the memory.

The last two chapters address the subject of fictional space in a more straightforward way and stray therefore further from architecture proper while moving closer to the real goal of the book. Painting offers more unfettered opportunity to spatial imagination than building, and I choose to follow one extended crisis in perception from late Gothic to the sixteenth century, which continues to spawn consequences in all the visual arts today. This is the enthralled discovery of, the ensuing disenchantment with, and the consequent undiscovering of the unified system of vision we call Renaissance perspective. If one had never known it, one wouldn't feel the loss.

A crucial irony is that scientific ways of seeing were the destructive force. I am not sure one can say whether the museum mentality was symptom or cause of the centrifugal, disintegrated vision which followed, and of which El Greco and Bruegel are my exemplars. In this book there isn't really space to mount the argument which the importance of the subject deserves, but my preliminary sense is that it is the antiquarian, cataloguer, or anatomist's view of the external world which eventually makes the approach espoused by this book possible. We are late descendants of Renaissance science.

The book ends in the most problematic place, reaching toward impossibility. If the next step beyond anything we have yet considered is the unbuildable, the one beyond that is the inconceivable, which we try to represent with some of Kafka's sketches.

Defining the unbuildable turns out to be harder than one could have foreseen. Certain things which exist are more farfetched than many which don't. And actual buildings can be fictional, which is to say uninhabitable and thus unrealizable, in certain specifiable ways.

Before long one comes to think that various ways of struggling against physical unlikelihood are more interesting and a truer illustration of this idea than simple non-existence. One gets used to things which at first looked impossible without ever understanding how they were achieved, yet there are certain effects, like the dome of St Paul's, which however long they are around, however exceeded in size by later buildings, will continue to astonish, for reasons which have more to do with the construction of the human mind than with the technical feats on which they are based.

Acknowledgments

GRATEFUL acknowledgement is made to University College of the University of Toronto, and especially Peter Heyworth and Peter Richardson, where a version of this material appeared as the Teetzel Lectures for 1986. Also to the Architectural Association School of Architecture and its Chairman, Alvin Boyarsky, for supporting them in an earlier form, to Peter Salter for telling me about structures, and finally to Robin Middleton for setting the project in motion as a book.

CHAPTER I

Gardens

ALL art is perishable; the canvases, languages, and customs on which it is built are slowly decaying, but gardens disappear faster than the others. Thus it is that no sixteenth-century ones survive intact, only twentieth-century reconstructions based on printed sources. Certainly our standards of authenticity must be more flexible in these precincts. A visitor to most cathedrals will see fresh stone inserted at intervals among the old. To more instructed observers the hand of the improver will be more evident, but someone who sees it only now may suppose modern bolsterings to be genuinely medieval clumsiness, and later intrusions may be lost in the welter of detail: how many tourists have picked out the portraits of nineteenth-century restorers stuck on the west front of Laon cathedral?

In gardens we are content with a lower quotient of ancientness. The life of reliable building stone is measured in centuries; few plant species outlast the human span, and when they do, overstep the bounds they were originally set. Scrupulosity has produced some gardens which contain only plants popular in Shakespeare's (or Pope's, or Josephine Bonaparte's) time, but not raised by Elizabethan, Augustan or Napoleonic methods. Looking at sixteenth-century plant embroidery one is inclined to believe that these species *grow* differently now, that a more heraldic vision of plants influenced how they were potted, trimmed, or encouraged, and that therefore essential features of past gardens will be missing from our carefully-nurtured models of then.

Not that it is futile to strive for these reenactments. The parterres at Versailles and the maze at Hampton Court, though rebuilt, are the most vivid reminders we have of their creators' relation to the universe, and thus key monuments in the history of art and consciousness. We have come to think that we are nearer to seventeenth-century courtiers watching them at play in bosky alleys, than involved in pompous ceremonies in the mirror lined rooms of the palace. This belief is kin to our strange new preference for proletarian over ministerial history. Peripheries and anonymities are realer than centres and notabilities, which seem obvious and unmysterious. In the broadest terms this is another manifestation of the movement of thought and feeling which prompted the English garden as a counter to the French.

Coming from a different culture our view might be different, but for us there are really two kinds of garden. Ever since the eighteenth century there have been formal and informal, French and English, or classic and Romantic; and with them are linked political and social ideas as well: constraint and freedom, authoritarian rule and democracy. Yet when we look closer at either of these two we find some interfusion of qualities: the spontaneous English form is more artful and the rigid French more fluid than the code appears to permit.

At Sceaux for example, a Le Nôtre garden near Paris which survives without its palace (demolished at the Revolution), we see 'trees cut to statues, statues thick as trees' according to Pope's beautiful vision which readers have understandably taken as a condemnation of this style of fierce control of the vegetable world. But his line lingers in memory because it expresses so vividly a metamorphic confusion between art and nature which, barring – at this late date – actual appearances of the divinity among our woods and streams, is our truest magic and nearest approach to a higher range of reality.

Yews at Sceaux are cut to columns and make a roofless architecture framing a perfectly rectangular pool. Or so it looks from afar: coming nearer we find that the long runway of water has hexagonal ends and a cross-arm initially hidden from us, which makes a trip down one side much longer than the other. Regularities in gardens dissolve when one is immersed in them. Each of the cone-yews is already taking its own course even if trimmed yesterday. One grows too fast, another turns brown and the straight lines will be ragged before the gardener passes by again.

The water's edge transmogrifies in a more unexpected way still. This body seems to grow or contract as we turn its corners, as breezes disturb the reflections which fall over its edges like dough which won't fit in the pan. Our memory of the clear outline we saw from afar is all that makes the experience a laboratory of sensation and saves us from getting lost in a wilderness of shadows.

At least that is how it is on days when the clouds are moving quickly across the ponds. For like other gardens the Versailles-type are very dependent for their effect on chances of weather. Their rooflessness is a fantastic freedom, to be large, ungainly, irresponsible, and also an acknowledgment of powerful forces which elude any control they exercise.

The garden of Sceaux, near Paris, with its rows of clipped yews – 'trees cut to statues'.

Le Nôtre and his contemporaries increased the scale of the gardens which preceded them. At the same time they simplified the component elements, two developments which have usually been seen as moves toward heartless clarity. But if one forgets the plan a little and gives oneself up to the moment, one will recognize Le Nôtre as one of the great psychologizers of space, the practitioner of a modern art of discontinuity.

Even the most dictatorial gardens of this type sometimes unsettle the observer with arrangements like optical illusions. At Rambouillet substances trade places with each other in an unnerving way: the part of gravel is suddenly taken by water, and the incomplete actions of marble figures trail off into the void. Now it is too late to go back on this vision, but perhaps the mental subversions of these gardens would still lie unperceived were it not for figures like Eugène Atget, the great French photographer who is their best modern interpreter, verging nearest to pure surrealism in these unproblematic places.

His vision of St Cloud, Versailles, and Sceaux, which he visits in an ideal time before others are up – just after dawn – before or after the popular seasons for going outdoors – at the end of winter or onset of autumn – is full of longing and loss. Chalky figures strain across a shapeless expanse of water toward each other and a union which will not come to pass. Or a solitary stone observer, her back turned to us, laments

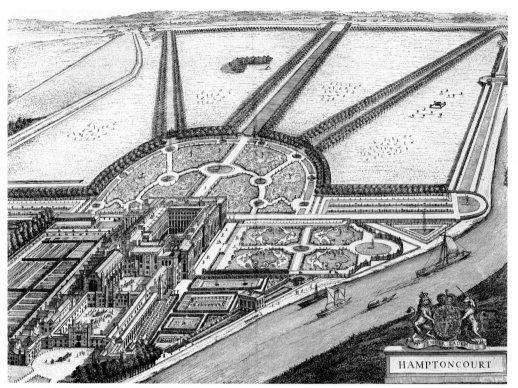

Bird's-eye view of Hampton Court Palace and its gardens, an engraving published in 1720 soon after the grounds were laid out.

the retreat of the water-mirror at her feet, which dries up and appears to pull away. Nature and art chase each other toward the same decay. Atget's contribution is to see them above all as places of passage, where one has leisure to note the tiniest flutterings of decline, where the slowing of time makes its inexorability more evident.

Even the most monotonous formal arrangements are to a certain perception fluid. Like an expressway the endless alleys at Caserta can feel a nightmare of motion or a perfect peace, either authoritarian imposition or oceanic wholeness. More than buildings, and for reasons perhaps obvious, the most carefully orchestrated gardens allow different readings. Even in highly structured societies, even in courts moving toward absolutism, gardens offer release. The bird's-eye views of Hampton Court show two entirely different experiences: coming and going, focus and dispersion. Leaving the palace one is confronted by paths radiating to a controlled infinity. When one gets to the end and turns around, or goes part way and turns round, everything is crushingly focused as by a burning glass. Now all walks lead to the same destination, indoors again. In this gigantic form the experience may be

Opposite: Two photographs of French gardens taken early in this century by Eugène Atget: St Cloud (*above*) and Sceaux (*below*).

monarchical oppression, but something like it waits for us at the end of
our visit to any compelling garden, however small. The illusion of
being at home in nature can be carried on so long and no longer. Even
one who 'works' in his own garden, that is, contributes to the fiction by
imitating agricultural labour, must at last confess the arbitrariness of
what he does and go back to more constrained activities. One's own
gardening is a special category of 'work' like Marie Antoinette's
attentions to her dairy herd. Perhaps somewhere a landowner has been
killed by a falling tree, swept away in a flood, or devoured by a bear
while taming his own patch of the earth's surface, but most of us can
only be civilizers in a fanciful sense of the word.

However true it may prove that all gardens have much the same thing
to say to us, the eighteenth-century English garden was one of the most
revolutionary ideas in the history of mankind. It is a kind of
organization which appears to be none, random dotting which still adds
up because it is subtly focal. At Stourhead in Wiltshire a beguiling
assortment of miniature structures emerges from among the trees
around the edges of the ragged central lake. Each ornament is from
certain vantages concealed or half concealed, but beyond the ample
spacing, there is little effort to conceal a frivolous diversity of style in
these pretend-houses. Formerly it was an even stranger zoo than now –

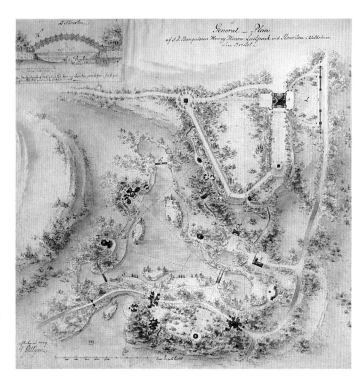

Stourhead, Wiltshire, with classical buildings emerging from an apparently natural landscape. *Left:* the Pantheon from across the lake. *Right:* plan by F.M. Piper showing the sophisticated but concealed artistry by which the various viewpoints are linked.

the root-house and Chinese hut among others have disappeared – but even today one can sit on the bench built into the front of the Gothic cottage and look across to a Pantheon remote enough to seem Roman instead of Lilliputian in scale, or to the grotto, most primitive shelter of all, a cave with rude punctures in the walls instead of windows, which frame by chance very telling views; or if one turns another way, to the reprieved village church (the village itself demolished and relocated over the brow where it interferes less with these ideal sylvan views) an authentic fragment of English history, a real not concocted memory but still an exhibit in this outdoor museum, a convenient jewel which is all we want of the old rural culture that went with it. Did villagers in picturesque costume occasionally troop over the rustic bridge to observe the passing in the churchyard of one of their number, who, buried there, became one of the owner's trophies, his stone another signpost to melancholy reflection? It *is* known and not a fanciful supposition that when he planned a tour of the garden its owner sent ahead a dependent in monkish garb to surprise his visitors (and serve them tea?) at the Gothic cot, as if there were actual hermits one could stumble across in one's passage through this landscape.

There is a revealing contemporary document, a plan of Stourhead drawn by a Swedish visitor in 1779, who also shows us in drawings of various views what an act of faith these gardens were. Trees which now swathe structures and landscape until all intentions are pleasingly veiled were in the eighteenth century meagre little whisps; then the groves were notional only, infant or at best adolescent.

The Swede's plan shows this garden's revolutionary relation to the owner's house: they were entirely out of sight of one another, the garden not an appendage or enhancement of the dwelling but a complete, separate world, as remote in its way from ordinary life as the false *hameau* at Versailles. Piper's diagram also makes clearer than a visit how relentless is the irregularity in the design of Stourhead. No Bavarian stuccoist ever hit on a more eccentric shape than the lake which controls the whole experience in this garden, as if someone had looked for the figure which would give maximum edge and minimum surface in the space available. The water is roughly triangular, but the three points are drawn out in serpentine extensions. Such English gardens make all Continental rococo, full of linear vagary and shredding, look tiny, like frightening waves decorating teacups.

At the University of Virginia Jefferson observed the same division we find at Stourhead, classical buildings, rococo gardens. Curves are allowed to run wild in serpentine walls, a controlled admission of wickedness back into Eden. It points up the rational control which makes almost all picturesque gardening experimental art in a limiting sense. Such gardens may have acted as goads to poets and painters, may have taunted artists in other mediums to admit more wildness to their vision, but they are in some sense safe places for dangerous mental explosions, far enough from real dwellings to insure the shock won't be directly felt.

In the woods, beside the lake, temples are naturalized. Taking one's place in the landscape, one could derive the creed these buildings are the calcified emanations of. At Shobdon in remote Herefordshire, an instructive manifestation survives of the symbiosis between the rococo garden and eighteenth-century religion. Bits of the previous, Roman-esque church were displaced to a neighbouring hillside to become a picturesque ruin consisting of three sculpted doorways strung together in a flimsy arcade, while back at the consecrated spot, a less weighty structure was substituted, starting from scratch. It is a house of worship like a boudoir, all fretwork and plaster, daintily flushed in ice cream colours.

These two poles of an effort to naturalize religion and disperse its mass into trellis-like concoctions which won't press too hard on the spectator find echoes in hut-temples all across Europe, the most famous, flagrant,

Marie Antoinette's *hameau*, or hamlet, in a corner of the park at Versailles, as remote from the palace as from real life.

and sobering being Marie Antoinette's *hameau* in the forest at the edge of the Trianon, itself at the edge of the formal gardens which extend from Versailles, a nested series of retreats that should have sounded an alarm.

As at Stourhead, some virtually functionless buildings are grouped around a lake, but in the French case more scenic, sustained, and hence unreal. For here the buildings consistently mimic rural reality, forming a single agricultural hamlet, staffed by a few farmers who supervised the ladies' fantastic games. In the biggest and flimsiest of the mock-cottages the queen and the most privileged women in the land made butter and cheese in silver containers resting on marble counters, or more likely gave a few desultory turns and left the process to be completed by an underling. On the floor above, reached by a stair wrapped like a bit of ribbon around a feathery poplar, was a thatched ballroom. Such was the failure of their sense of decorum that they imagined work and play could be brought into painless proximity.

In the English garden dairies became a fad where ladies dabbled, without, as far as we can tell, the full French effrontery of entering peasanthood. English gardens at their silliest never make interconnected sets of errors like this French ideal realm. If they fall under a single spell (as opposed to many: all the architectural styles of the past) it is a dream of union with the landscape, built it may be (as Marxists have rushed to point out) on political suppressions, sweeping away realities which wouldn't amuse the wandering eye. It may be a vision which forgets or obscures how the landscape actually works, but it isn't founded on such aggressive misperceptions of the muser's own role in it.

Later developments in the style have been seen as further obscuring the real roots of these grand orderings of the countryside, or as bringing halcyon longings and everyday facts into closer alignment. Capability Brown's effect on the English garden was, through Herculean movements of vast amounts of earth and armies of trees, to make it disappear more fully into the surrounding terrain. So many landscapes with which he tampered survive, and the eye is so used to them, that he has probably made a key contribution to many people's idea of what the English countryside was always like.

Visiting an ambitious example like Bowood in Wiltshire, we can try to re-apprehend the novelty of his manipulations. It is a territory from which most signs have been gently erased, oddities of contour, abruptness or strangeness of planting, discontinuity of whatever kind. Single plants are not allowed to stand out, and for the first time in garden history the planting seems to take no notice of the house, not becoming markedly elaborate as it approaches it. That is the greatest artifice of all, that a carefully tailored territory should appear untouched. Perhaps one would have affronted Brown by pointing out that his naturalism perpetuated a man-made scene, but he probably knew it. For Capability Brown would have recognized true wildness.

At Bowood an adjacent density to Brown's diffusion survives in the form of the earlier grotto and cascade which is more like a complete landscape of unfriendly rock than an isolated incident in a strung out series (like the grotto at Stourhead). In Italy, which was its point of origin, this tumultuous phase is often more creaturized and hence more vividly demonic. Spouts are portrayed as a monster *spitting*; instead of a hole in the rock one finds a face with a mouth, which seems to materialize suddenly on the rockface. At Frascati, at Bomarzo, and elsewhere a walk-in grotto is seen as a huge howling head, a maw which swallows us, and may refuse to cough up its prey. In English grottoes explicit depictions of nature's hostility have disappeared.

These portrayals of primitive dwellings are more threatening in Italy, where one occasionally finds links with the underworld surviving in ordinary life, in the cave-like shelters dug from rock at Matera, or

Entrance to a picnic-
chamber at Bomarzo,
Italy, where sculpture is
used to evoke the hostile
forces of nature.

constructed without right angles or windows in the trulli scattered
across central Apulia.

Gardens which pick up such suggestions seem to enshrine superstition, to be prisons not refuges, resurrecting a time when the world
teemed with fears. They are the horror films or Gothic novels of
gardening art, where man teases himself with ideas of danger, curse, and
unfathomable wickedness.

At Bomarzo, the conflict raging beneath the surface between benign
and hostile forces takes shape as intertwined gigantic figures, halluci-
nated and then coaxed forth in natural outcroppings of limestone. We
are torn between finding them the least or the most artificial of all
garden statues. Dragons which emerge from the ground like effusions
of an unfavourable soil fertile with troubles, are advocates for a certain
view of nature, more insistent than ordinary Floras or Zephyrs.

Interestingly enough, savage gardens seem less likely to last; there is
more danger they will revert to unclaimed or undifferentiated thicket,
as if it were harder to hang onto the sense of a shaping vision there. Some
interesting relics survive, however, outside literature and painting
where one is more used to them, of the new eighteenth-century love
affair with wildness.

There is the bark hut by a waterfall in North Wales which Dr Johnson's friend Worthington built for taking tea in. Rather abruptly the very landscapes shunned by earlier travellers – Wales, the Lake District, the Highlands – became prized as the last refuges of something which was being chased off the earth, Nature in its primeval vigour before it felt the smoothing hand of man. The Italian foretastes of this enthusiasm for natural sublimity and violence had appeared, like their English successors, in a claustrophobically overrefined cultural phase. Urbanites like Dr Johnson and indoorsmen like Thomas Gray give us the early appreciations of the Hebrides and the Alps.

The idea that one could incorporate the most awestruck moments of one's life with nature in a garden proved rather perishable. Victorian gardens forewent this captive wildness, but their relinquishment now seems a real loss, and we view more indulgently early naive manifestations like Batty Langley's rhapsody offered to the idea of the serpentine line, from afar like some kind of folk art. If anyone had been fool enough to build this gallery of mazes (but how serious was Batty? was it more like a list of possible forms than a single coherent design?) he would have found it less a joking matter when enmeshed in its coils. Batty's tangles are rococo curves as neurosis, diagrams of anxiety which one no longer contemplates, but *lives*, through protracted moment after moment.

In spite of this resemblance (both forms mislead the visitor, perverting the Path) eighteenth-century serpentine walks are not simple lineal descendants of earlier mazes. A maze is too intricate a form of disorder to appeal to eyes which relish the Alps.

Mazes are in fact one of the rare features which have recently become detached from gardens and led an independent existence. This revived enthusiasm after centuries of disuse, is it metaphysical queasiness extending even to art, which becomes almost impossible except in whimsical or undercut forms? For mazes are the mind turning back on itself and bad temperedly biting its own tail.

Like recent conceptual art, the maze is a form which sets up a great divide between perpetrator and victim. From the adjacent artificial hilltop it seems as clear as a wiring diagram. But once one comes down and submits, one's superiority is lost and it becomes a cruel and befuddling hoax. Isn't it surprising there aren't stories of murders in mazes, committed by those driven to distraction, circling back on earlier thoughts and finally overpowered by paranoid delusion which sees enemies everywhere?

The concision of Japanese gardens make them cousins of the monomaniacal maze, with this proviso: though just as conceptual as the

A page from Batty Langley's
New Principles of Gardening,
1728, a series of experiments in
serpentine lines and mazes.

maze, they are not especially puzzle-like. Japanese naturalism is alien to
the West, as if constructed for senses of different focal length. To bring
one's attention to bear on vegetable and mineral textures as intently as
that, seems a kind of madness to us, foregoing the individuated self in
order to know what it feels like to be moss.

A moss garden in Kyoto eliminates all discordant tones and surrounds
us with bumpy beds of moss in a grove made from a single species of
tree, with all the distracting lower branches removed. The slyest
subtlety here is that standards of comparison have been pruned away,
forcing us to seek worlds of variety in the monotonous moss.

And if one stops before it long enough, one does indeed find it rising
and falling, becoming sparse or lush, letting a rock break through or
covering it, and containing all possibility in itself. If one were alone, one
would sink down beside the moss, watch ants set out on thousand-mile

journeys, and see lifetime after lifetime stretching off within the small plot as one does in Chinese painting or Kafka's stories. Perhaps it is a saving concession to decorum that one permits oneself these treks only at a double remove. To find the world in a grain of sand one must become a speck, for a minute which lasts years, but without yielding up one's actual height, one's suspended impatience.

Doubtless this is a Western view of Japanese gardens. If we knew the length of the longest (or the average) Japanese visit to such a place, we would know something further about how they succumb to their gardens. The most overtly metaphysical Japanese garden, Ryoan-ji at Kyoto, of all the world's landscapes most like a philosophical text, takes a strictly controlled number of elements and arranges them in a stultifyingly clear pattern like a map, leaving each individual so untrimmed that each is a little dose of wildness. So the wide blank sheet on which chaos is displayed may, in some moods, be quite other than a comfort.

Moss garden of Saiho-ji Temple, Kyoto, Japan. Over a hundred kinds of moss are placed with calculated naturalness.

Zen garden of Ryoan-ji, Japan: rocks and raked sand arranged as objects of meditation.

This is to take these spaces tragically, and wrongheadedly, for even without being told, we sense they enshrine a connoisseurship of raggedness. One can be fussiest of all about one's disorder, and the fifteen rocks in their five clumps at Ryoan-ji are examples without equal of man's tyranny over nature. Here chaos holds still forever, and the observer moves carefully round it, to see it outlined first one way and then another, against peeling walls like the graph of a sunset which took years to dissolve. Everything is a sign of passage, yet in this secure compound, change not permanence is the illusion. True, accidents of light alter the forms, but one can come back tomorrow and will find the same unmanaged shapes held perfectly in place.

So the courageous meditation on Nothing which this strange little world strikes a Westerner as being, is gilded by complacency. All these crazy outlines have been thumbed so often that, without losing their actual irregularity, they are smoothed in thought to the consistency of prayer beads, not a true universe but another stylization.

The more one looks at any Japanese garden the more calculation one sees, the less true necessity. All the bridges are real bridges, and the

27

islands real islands in the sense that the first really cross water and the second are really surrounded by it, but since the islands are invented, the links which run between them are hoaxes. A path wanders toward a shore, and suddenly there is a hewn stone to mark a landing place, dishevelment and then a sharp edge – one is never left alone long before being brought up against some mild refinement on a natural shape.

In the garden at one of the imperial villas a large pavilion looks out at three small islands in the shape of Japan, too tiny to be visited, fulfilled in being seen. Perhaps Western miniatures and models are connected more with children because viewed as arenas for at least mock-activity. Opposite the perfect spectacle, the Japanese building too is a pure contemplative, a viewing platform, almost as if part of the mechanism of sight itself, the eye-frame or eye-lid. Like some other forms of refinement the Japanese relation to nature seems a specialization as well, freeing *and* disabling, because so many acts are not allowed for in it.

Seventeenth-century European gardens were nearer to Japanese in some aspects than they have been since, in their enjoyment of strict management which makes things look like other things, not according to any cosmic scheme but in unorganized love of artifice. English topiary is the last word in imposing geometric perfection on plants. Cypresses are cone-like, certain shrubs approximate spheres, and it is only a short step to trim the fast growing box into more complicated shapes in which it continues to look comfortable, and thus we get large green dragons, peacocks, toadstools and corkscrews.

Early twentieth-century prints of Levens Hall in Westmorland show what incongruities were tolerated in the high flush of Arts and Crafts enthusiasm for this revived feature of old gardens. Discordant forms jostle each other, and the sense of scale has gone violently awry. A large green mushroom sits beside a green cottage of approximately equal height; one is seeing elements taken from a formal garden, picturesquely grouped.

Sometimes the jumble is like a warehouse or shop, making us wish that hedge-creatures could be dotted more sparingly and other less insistent transformations prevail. Hedge-architecture is the best of these imitations – walls, doorways, and windows in a tiny-leaved material, which is the vegetable equivalent of pebbledash. Wobbly renditions of stability seem more profound than frozen versions of lively facts like birds. Here we accept that no right angle will be true, and all walls helplessly battered.

It is one of the world's stranger facts that an influential version of architectural history chose plants as the models for and in a special sense

Topiary at Levens Hall, Westmorland, a wood engraving of 1901.

the original components of buildings. Attempting to demonstrate his theory of the origin of Gothic forms in vegetable behaviour, Sir James Hall produced the famous Willow Cathedral, which appears to us, contrary to its nurse's wish, a preposterous attempt to force young trees to behave Gothically. The fact that the most pliant plants if caught early enough can be trained into architectural shapes is no more informative than that feet can be bound or human lips have plates inserted in them. Hall might have taken warning from the practice of espaliering fruit trees, which was never an attempt to uncover their true nature.

Rationality aside, it was a powerful dream which read back into buildings lost hopes for them. If only they could be again, as we imagine they once were, flexible, whole, and responsive like creatures. To the enthusiast, Gothic buildings were both perfect in an unthought-out way and about to become even better or at least not yet full grown.

Hall's building which is alive wasn't a garden ornament but a serious archaeological experiment. Placing such ideological weight on the roots of Gothic, his generation showed that, for them, history had assumed new power – historical explanations took one straight to essences.

Essays in rusticity. *Left:* an early 18th-century attempt to relate Gothic architecture to natural forms, the 'Willow Cathedral'. *Right:* Ernest Gimson's library at Bedales School, Hampshire, 1911.

For us it remains not far removed from a children's tree-hut, but perhaps the persistence of attempts to reintroduce such rudeness in architecture shows it isn't a groundless fantasy, and prompts one to think that in many buildings where we never become aware of it as a motive, some of their power derives from reversion to natural forms, Hawksmoor's massiveness, Lutyens' humpiness, Peruzzi's tangled darkness being signs in architects not blatantly organic of profound indebtedness to landscape-sensations. Though it might be most interesting of all to trace organic promptings in obscure effusions like these, the line of consciously reversionary builders is a revealing strand too, even if its main monuments are curiosities not masterpieces.

The English Arts and Crafts designer Ernest Gimson built a small number of houses like burrows and schools like barns. They are extremely scarce because so relentlessly handcrafted and so unconcessive to public taste that they remained cult objects. It is an un-amusing paradox that Arts and Crafts reimmersion in simple work and folk tradition should have led to a Utopia where each chair and hanging cost the earth.

30

So Gimson's are dream buildings, his library for Bedales the best and the craziest, reassimilating civilization to rustic ways. The other supreme monument of the movement is Lethaby's church at Brockhampton in remote Herefordshire, a jewel of painstaking childishness, located so naturally and un-urbanly that few are ever going to see it, a rose born to blush unseen.

The greatest Continental descendant of Ruskin and of the Arts and Crafts effort to creaturize and thus in a special way to individualize buildings did not hide his works away in the countryside. Gaudi built a good deal, most of it in the heart of a large city, Barcelona. But his kind of naturalism is more extreme than any English version. Energy as he embodies it is always monstrous and life is thrusting on toward decadence.

Gaudi interests us more than other Art Nouveau architects because the monstrosity in his work is far from superficial, a vision which has deeply infected the way the spaces are constructed; but he is often at his best when freest, on rooftops and in parks, making imaginary spaces, not efficiently but only imaginatively habitable ones, not much more

Form released from function: the roofscapes of Gaudi's Casa Mila, Barcelona (*above*) and topiary work at Ansouis, in Provence.

A pavilion, more
symbolic than usable, on
the terrace of Montacute,
a Jacobean house in
Somerset.

usable than hedge riddles found in the typical Mannerist garden
precincts, like so many of Gaudi's, where a quiet preference for
monstrosity prevails.

At one of these, Ansouis in Provence, the barest means produce the
most vivid impossibilities. These gardens are built on presently
unfunctional bits of rampart; out of hedge are constructed a lot of tiny
unenterable rooms in inaccessible places, suspended above the true
ground several storeys beneath, like an idea which hasn't yet found its
earthly feet. The detachment from use which Mannerist conceits share
with Gaudi's excrescences suggests an unexpected link between these
disparate styles, both advocating autonomy for the formal imagination.

In another great Renaissance garden, at Montacute, notional pavilions are stuck on a wall like houses on a bridge, which remain carbuncles
however charming on an alien body which performs an overriding
function in which they can't share.

These places are so conceited and in some important sense so barren
that occasionally they must have been denied the name of garden
altogether. In the wrong mood one can see them as elaborate thwarting-

33

mechanisms and no more, anti-patterns which mount an attack on life. Thus at Villandry one experiences mainly denial, among a lot of scraps of hedge like a tailor's waste basket, leftovers from what might have been a set of usable paths before they were jolted into this confusion. Here we find a whole range of disorganizations, and a variety of vantages for mastering or succumbing to them. From surrounding humped up 'ramparts', or from upper storeys of the house, one gets one's precious bird's-eye views, in which all the ground level perversity is beautifully justified.

Later history has not made these gardens easier to appreciate, casting them as heartless fictions, but it did finally produce some fascinating hybrids which redeem the debt of the intervening century or two of incomprehension. In the early twentieth century the loving travesties infused with real stodginess which Lutyens was producing on the architectural styles of the past had their equivalent in the gardens he and Gertrude Jekyll contrived for his comically monstrous houses like their frivolous shadows.

At Hestercombe, a Lutyens garden without a Lutyens house – it is not really strange that his best garden arose where it needed to do all the work of architecture and not just echo a powerful master on the premises – the axial plan is continually transgressed by the plants. These gardens are a gentle war between two strong forces, an unyielding geometry arranged so profligately that sphere is followed by square, bounded by cylinder, overlaid by triangle; and a vigorous growth which can't be contained within these drawn lines. Gertrude Jekyll came to prefer plants with the boldest outlines and fiercest thrusts, and came to use a small number of species in large clumps so that differences in height and texture from their neighbours stood starkly forth like outspoken conversation. Only thus did she feel able to contest the space with Lutyens' witty patterns, and between them they imparted a force to formal garden design unimaginable before.

A more modest and famous effort of a similar kind, the garden at Sissinghurst, has learned that the secret for enlivening regular plans is violation. One creates path upon path, meaning to let every one of them grow closed. Plants are given their head, after being required to make absurd submissions. In one corner of Sissinghurst only white ones are allowed, and this has become the most popular part of the garden, the most allegorical, man's creations the ghosts of nature's.

Sissinghurst offers a crystallized form of the conflict seen at its most sublimated in eighteenth-century gardens like Stowe, where the ordering power of man is sometimes almost imperceptible. The shaping

The early 20th-century gardens which signal a partial return to formality: Hestercombe in Somerset (*above*) and Sissinghurst in Kent (*below*).

The gardens of Chiswick Villa, near London, laid out by William Kent for Lord Burlington. The tempietto faces an obelisk in the centre of a round pond originally surrounded by potted orange trees.

force on the Grecian Valley at Stowe is so subtle that one may feel one is hallucinating it, and supplying the formal ideas oneself. The main stimulus to perception here is the Temple of Concord and Victory which closes one end of the valley, that nearest the house. Its presence almost justifies one in thinking the shallow bowl of the landscape is a votive offering presented at a shrine, in the same ritual of reconciliation between nature and culture, country and city, which is usually more demonstrative, at Chiswick for example where the round pond before the round temple ringed by potted orange trees pruned to spheres all take part in a sacrament of the circle, preaching the oneness of man and nature, the main perception that gardens offer us, making them the reservoir of some of our fondest hopes.

CHAPTER II

Monuments

THOUGH both are largely freed from function, monuments and gardens represent opposite ends of the whole range of architecture. Monuments are more or less monstrous exaggerations of the requirement that architecture be permanent, and gardens are the furthest reach of man's constructive energies evading this necessity. Of course lasting power depends on other things besides sturdiness – for example, on whether people continue to want the stone or metal eminence. Strength can be an incitement to wreck. Castles and fortifications have probably been more often deliberately disabled ('slighted' is the funny expression for this) than other kinds of construction.

Apparently of all the vast number of carved and cast images of Stalin which graced squares from one end of the Soviet Union to the other, only one survives, in his birthplace, from which someone occasionally imagines the cult spreading again. There are now no official images of Stalin, still a strangely well-known face, but there is no shortage in Russia today of iconic features glaring down at one. A photo from the Russian colony at Spitzbergen in the Arctic shows what an essential part of the furniture of life these oversized detached heads are. Here Lenin's dome adds to the surrounding snow-glare. Even the most serious student of monuments would need to undergo prolonged residence in a place saturated with such intimidations to understand the force of one of the most hallowed forms of memorial, the Colossus.

A history of toppled monuments might be the most interesting of all, but very hard to tell, because often a studied effort removes the literary and pictorial traces as well as the masses of rock. Presumably combing Soviet periodicals of the 1930s, late 40s and early 50s one could fill in many gaps in the visual record of Stalin's deification, but maybe a taboo operates which inhibits overrecording of these feats, at least immediately.

And in any case, is it the truth or simply the falsehood of a society which one learns from its monuments? Perhaps not even a revealing kind of falsehood, because diverse societies express themselves in the same exhausted vocabulary, an impoverished brand of speech. For us these columns, arches (entrances to nowhere), temples and colossi are essentially 'classical', but maybe it is simply that antique civilization (and especially Roman) was unusually focused on permanence.

Serious tourists are perhaps monumentalizing the landscapes they pass through, classicizing them by concentrating on certain nodes of significance which acquire ceremonial eminence even if only remarkable barns or abandoned factories (and how much more easily if little-visited churches). The tourist's objects of interest become in some manner *unused*, even when he conscientiously imagines their former lives. His activity is always reconstructive: in medieval cathedrals one medievalizes, that is to say makes them into memorials to their first inhabitants.

But one is touchy about this and likes to do it invisibly, preferring that no one else in the vicinity should be doing it too, as one prefers to visit a grave without a lot of company. Cemeteries are crowded but unbusy places. Most monuments seek or are accorded the contrary of these two conditions, wide empty spaces around and plenty of passing traffic.

Many monuments make a positive feature of such lack of company or of content. In fact a main archetype of the monument is a featureless hulk or picture of emptiness on which the attention is paradoxically concentrated. One of the great preachers of pure monumentality, the Austrian designer Adolf Loos, has been accorded a tomb like a pinnacle of uncommunicative strength. It is the nearest thing to an unmarked block, raised on a little platform to show it is a finished act, not raw material waiting to be carved. But this starkness of expression, the equivalent in art of a Northern heath, instead of standing, as most monuments dream of doing, alone in the world, resembles the average building crushed into a city street, because it is one of row upon row of markers in a large urban cemetery.

Among the beauties of this lump is its person-sized scale, like an abstract version of the missing fact. As a rule we expect monuments to overreach themselves, growing too big until they tower over all of humanity left behind. The subtlest version of this is Lutyens' Cenotaph in Whitehall, which is only an imaginary tomb, containing no actual or nameable remains and reversing the common sensible proportions between casket and pedestal. It depicts a coffin translated entirely into stone, hoisted needlessly high on a towering base like a column of rectangular plan, as if the casket in its strained aspiring had created an elongated version of its own self.

Images of death. *Left:* Lutyens's Cenotaph in Whitehall, London, *Right:* Holzmeister's entrance to Vienna Crematorium.

The long sides of the base are softened by rows of flags, an unwilling concession by Lutyens to mundane reality and ceremonies made of living participants: his design called for the flags as well to be carried out in stone, which would have preserved better the unattainable ideality of his construction.

Its greatest subtleties are practically invisible. It contains no straight lines: the sides curve toward convergence so gently they would meet 1000 feet above the ground. The top and bottom echo the earth's curvature and assimilate this monument's flagrant verticality to the soil again. These lines, segments of circles whose centres are 900 feet below ground, secretly bury all the apparent defiance of last necessities. It is an object which underpins the nominal intransigence of monuments with a final yielding where it really counts.

Lutyens' 'building' is downward tending in spite of itself. Of course it has always been one of the vividest graphs of death to frame us in shapes which crush us, like the awful maw which acts as the main portal to the central crematorium in Vienna. This is not a vision of vaporization as the last bodily stage, but of an intolerable heaviness, features erased, all openings looking as if they will close in some final shutting-down.

Christo, one of the most ingenious and absurd 'conceptual artists' (a semantic blunder) has thought of a way of turning pompous buildings into corpses. His 'Wrapped Reichstag' is one of the most powerful of these because it begins with an inartistic hulk which rouses mixed feelings in the observer. As a reminder from a hateful past (a pawn used by Hitler mopping up his opponents) the old Reichstag building is probably the focus of a certain amount of aggression. But there has also been a (perhaps misguided) effort to see it as a sign of a new, chastened Germany rising from the ashes. So in wrapping or blanking out this monument Christo undoes a lot of pious or self-serving effort to resurrect a tarnished idea. It is not just any old mummy but a nation entombed.

Hitler's plans for this city if they had ever come to pass would have wrapped or anesthetized its architectural expression in a more expensive, less superficially messy way. One says this complacently, yet realizes with dismay that the noblest as well as the shabbiest public conceptions seem to be suited by similarly numbing kinds of expression.

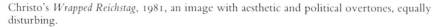

Christo's *Wrapped Reichstag*, 1981, an image with aesthetic and political overtones, equally disturbing.

The Lincoln Memorial, Washington, wrapped in columns representing the states of the Union.

The Lincoln Memorial in Washington is wrapped in columns like anonymity, and is almost never seen without the long reflecting pool, its ghost. But before one makes this the archetype of uncommunicative monumentality, one must look round in this city of monuments, perhaps the largest conglomerate on the earth which has any hope of achieving the dream of being pure commemoration, an enormous living cemetery.

For Washington has memorials more chilling than Lincoln's; after all, the columns in that temple each have personal names, which are written over them. Each one is a state of the union, and there are thirty-six, the number of states when Lincoln was President, which were the great supports of the idea of union he fervently defended. A more truthful monument would have found a way of representing architecturally the determined effort by eleven of these to leave the building. Like many others this monument represents an interesting conflict as stasis.

It is described by the National Park Service as the equal of the great antiquities of Greece and Rome. Its main competitor, the proposal by John Russell Pope, was more Mesopotamian, a pyramidal ziggurat: at the top of a mound as tall as the Washington Monument was perched a temple the size of the present Lincoln Memorial.

The National Gallery of Art, Washington, 1937–40: the classical tradition as elegant blankness.

It is one of the most fascinating and horrible things of its kind ever put forward. Pope went on to design some of the most interesting buildings in Washington, the National Archives, National Gallery of Art, the Jefferson Memorial, each serving a symbolic function, each marked by a combination of feminine sleekness and blank expanses suggestive of the tomb. Of these, only Archives breaks into surface sculpture and runs away with itself in inscribed words. To someone who stops to read its lengthy inscriptions it seems a verbose affair even before he sees a single one of its immense collection of documents. Yet the main architectural expression moves in another direction than pointless garrulity. Towering over the building's pediments is a rectangular solid of masonry, unbroken, windowless, and suggesting that the classical dress of the ground storey is a coating or curtain around a more primitive core, as if the accumulated weight of history has caused all the documents to fuse into a single indivisible block. National unity is best expressed by this: the past is current as a sleeping giant which no one would dream of disturbing.

Pope's most magnificent projects were carried out, if not conceived, during the Second World War, and were perhaps more than we are allowed to remember by their present guardians, a conscious answer to the megalomaniac Fascist and Nazi projects. Hitler's first completion of this kind, the Haus der Deutschen Kunst in Munich (now the *Deutschen*

The Haus der Kunst, Munich, a form of classicism into which it is easy to read totalitarian meanings.

has gone from the title) reminds an American visitor of Washington, but goes further. Here is an 'endless' row of columns like the faceless integers of a totalitarian crowd, of an army above all, now quietly put forward as an ideal of social organization. This is the clean and orderly Germany that the builder could guarantee if we would obey. Many were doubtless duly impressed that such coercion made its first full dress architectural appearance in a museum lording it over painting and sculpture.

As these buildings present columns in an ideal crowd, military cemeteries realize an ideal form of the cemetery, in which the dead are really a crowd, all killed at the same time in the same way. They are, even symbolically, inert places with little reminder of the violence which brought them into being. Only their locations do not form part of an ideal arrangement, because dictated by necessity, for battles will not ordinarily occur in accessible places on the primary tourist routes, yet remoteness becomes a strange value in itself.

One of the most distant and impressive commemorates a long, indecisive, and costly campaign among the lower ranges of the Italian Alps in the First World War. Like most battles this one has been given a resounding name as if it had taken place on the mountain top, Monte Grappa, where the memorial now is. But the twenty thousand corpses which this mountain is said to contain were collected from far afield to

43

be formed into this multitudinous monument. Here, Cyclopean masonry competes with the mountain underneath by echoing its form, erecting a human mound on the larger natural one. The immense 'building' consists of six receding circular tiers, within which each person is expressed as a minute void, in rows of round-headed holes like the non-individual work of insects. Many other memorials de-individualize the integers, but nowhere else are emptiness and forceful-ness so mysteriously conjoined: a giant hill made by collecting nullities, a large presence of vivid absences.

The memorial's plan shows that the designers of the Fascist period were not content to leave it at that: this comet has a tail: the tranquil hump is joined to a processional way which runs 300 yards along a ridge to the smaller Austrian memorial posed on an adjoining height. It isn't uncommon for monuments to back away from their most uncompro-mising assertions. Even the pyramids probably had little roads leading toward them and little caretaker's booths or depots near their bases. It would be a frightening idealist who asked that the Monte Grappa mound hold the mountain top alone, without access routes, without proposing any activity to visitors, destroying the traces of how it arose as if its builders had come out of and reascended into the clouds.

The processional way calls forth events which match these structures. There is an ideal of social life, realized better in 1930s' Germany than Italy it would seem, in which never ending or frequent parades are the transcendent activity, pompous, automatic, and enervating, at least for the spectators who experience an unreflective catharsis.

Visits to military memorials are not fervent in the way attending a parade is supposed to be, but in the societies which favour them they seem to spawn odd emotions. Soviet weddings often end in a ceremony of re-dedication at each town's monument to the Great Patriotic War, as Russians have christened the Second, as if to exacerbate their feelings at every mention, keeping partisan involvement alive.

The American attitude toward the battlefields of the Civil War of just over a century ago is similarly mysterious. They are surprisingly popular loci of tourism. Perhaps there is a shortage of such sites and memories: wars have not often been fought on American soil, a boast, a regret, a matter of unconscious perplexity. Americans do not feel particularly safe any more, but their territory is still inviolable in a different way from that of others. There is no American parallel to the chain of Napoleonic forts on the south coast of England; missile installations aren't designed to impress observers on the ground.

Attitudes toward the American Civil War are still perplexed, and not

Memorial to the Italian dead of the First World War at Monte Grappa.

only in the South where it has until recently consumed more energy than it does in the North. Predictably, for the losers will necessarily concern themselves more with the struggle's consequences than the victors do, as shown over and over, by the Welsh and the English or Bretons and French, among others.

Contrary to what schoolchildren are told, that civil wars are worst of all, where brother fights brother, they are, at sufficient distance, by far the best of all, for the symbol hunter. This particular war has entered the national imagination as the great acting out of the central conflicts in the American temperament, between principle (N) and expediency (S), head and heart, industry and agriculture, future and past, shallow right and venerable wrong, countinghouse and warm community. The most powerful version of the war's significance, irrational but widespread, is a melancholy one: from that day the path was chosen and the country opted for rationality, and thus all the strengths of rooted traditional life were permanently foregone. Americans can no longer be members of a community, they are carpet-baggers shifting opportunistically about on the surface of the earth, pursuing profit and self-fulfillment.

Some preface of this kind is necessary to understand the American involvement in sites like the battlefield at Gettysburg. Of all landscapes the one at Gettysburg is most thoroughly ruled by monuments, not arranged in formal or culminating groups but scattered over the hillsides. Such is the ideology of the place that they must not feel graceful, as in a picturesque English park. For they have a higher duty than any aesthetic one: they are markers, and must adhere to precise spots, where a charge was repelled or a battery stood. Except of course that these were matters of conjecture by the time the monuments got built (the first ones appearing six years after the battle, a flood which has continued at varying pace ever since) so that principles of design or anti-design have played a part even if sometimes unconsciously.

One of the oddest features is that many of the monuments face away from the observer, the observer sticking to the ceremonial route made of old farm lanes, that is. On an ordinary day that is the only kind of observer there is. The more serious kind who retraces the movements of combatants must be the equivalent of those who clamber over cathedral roofs with their measuring tapes.

Some of these monuments aim at a degree of reenactment: occasionally one comes over the brow of a hill and looks down the sights of a prone bronze sharpshooter, as if the whole thing was a giant diorama trying to put you in foot soldiers' shoes. Yet the illusion is terribly incomplete. One is asked to imagine creeks running red with blood, and the noise and confusion of battle, while around one is the most torpid farmland weighed down by summer heat.

And truly the standard monumental vocabulary is a million miles from the experience of slaughter. No one seems to know the architects of any of the monuments, though some are buildings in their own right, like the series of New York memorials in craggy castellated form, denizens of Central Park rather than backwoods Pennsylvania. One's attention is deflected onto stylizations of rudeness and architectural translations of heroism: rough masonry equals military virtues. The more interesting the monument the further it takes you from the battle.

One might even view the whole thing as an anthology of commemorative styles. Through accidents of politics this runs right up to the present. Most of the Southern states had stayed away until recently, making it basically a Northern memorial. But near the time of the centennial many of these states came round and commissioned memorials, resulting in a wonderful series beginning with the Georgia shrine of 1961 and continuing to the latest, Tennessee of 1982. Anyone who doubts that monuments can be powerful self-revelations even when pompous or absurd should study these, especially the florid Louisiana and Mississippi memorials, both by Donald DeLue (who decorated the front of the Philadelphia Post Office in a not-dissimilar style forty years earlier). These last two put unabashed sentiment into large bronze groups of Baroque complexity, like mammoth table centrepieces.

Gettysburg, USA, a battlefield transformed into a memorial park.

One tends to assume that monuments are regressive because public taste demands it. Doubtless piety is sometimes served by having one's monument look not quite up to date, if not definitely archaic, though this too is sought after in certain countries and climes – there are Russian war memorials tenanted by brutes from a Slav epic, and the Capitol in Ottawa still accumulates reliefs which could have been carved by a Mission Indian a hundred years ago.

Conscious archaism is one way of explaining the choice of a pyramid for a more or less person-sized grave mound, as at Blickling in Norfolk. By that date Egyptian culture was identified as a civilization of tombs, not the older, more unscrutable source of all knowledge (Egypt as seen by the ancient Greeks) so the shape seemed a melancholy, immobilized one, and presumably the optimistic Egyptian interpretation of it was unknown. In Egypt it was a diagram of the diffusion of life-giving heat and light by the sun, so, far from inert, sketched a transmission which continued, and made visible a ladder the deceased could climb.

Right: Mies van der Rohe's monument to the murdered Communist leaders Karl Liebknecht and Rosa Luxemburg in Berlin, 1926. *Opposite:* woodland cemetery surrounding the crematorium at Stockholm, by Asplund and Leverentz, 1935–40.

But whatever the metaphysical gloss of mounds, they are a hard form truly, and not just notionally or superstitiously, to animate. One of Mies van der Rohe's most original designs was the memorial to Karl Liebknecht and Rosa Luxemburg in Berlin, a dynamic mound and one of the most important twentieth-century contributions to the monumental repertoire. Studies for this monument show that it progressed through various more communicative phases before reaching the final form. It was originally conceived as a wall (the one against which the proletariat had been backed and from which it would propel itself like a spring under tension). In photomontage Mies tried out large inscriptions across its whole breadth and deployed speakers on perches built like podiums atop it. It does not seem a very practical idea that a cemetery will sow the seeds from which revolution will spring, though one can almost hallucinate before this monument a force which reaches from beyond the tomb to destabilize society. That is the meaning of this centrifuge of jagged forms as we see it, but if he held to the wall-idea, Mies' own view of its content was almost opposite. The effectiveness of the object is finally measured by its short life. The Nazis were so impressed with its power that they lost no time in destroying it: it lasted a bare seven years.

Certainly vandal-proofing couldn't have had much to do with the forms devised for the crematorium and surrounding burial ground in Stockholm, but among other things this barely perceptible monumentality would be very hard to erase. We have gone from the pyramid, the ultimate in shaped and stylized mounds, to Mies's Cubistic disruption of the mound, like the energy of the dead reerupting among the living, to this melted conclusion in Sweden, a protrusion which feels like the last remnant of something. This is the ultimate in subliminal memorials, where clumps of trees speak faintly of those buried beneath, by drifting gently across a slight bulge made by the massed presence of the dead. Trees are avatars of the departed, a more primitive form of their spirit; death is a regression to cruder kinds of organization.

Richard Long's ideas bear a similar relation to architecture. Sometimes one isn't sure whether one of his piles of stones naturalizes the art-prompting, or voices a final disillusion with constructions more focused than this. We find the idea in a collapsed form, in an unlikely place, to which we will not and are not meant to come. We know about the work only because he has decided to tell us. It is reduced to hearsay, a ghost. Yet hearsay, it turns out, is realer than some things.

A Thousand Stones Added to the Footpath Cairn by Richard Long, 1974: minimal architecture.

Christo's more extensive, disruptive, and evanescent works are usually over-documented like a civilization (was there ever one like this?) which kept voluminous records of a life it didn't actually lead. Endless photos assure us that the Running Fence actually took place, yet it remains even so, even now, improbable.

This fence was a deliberately cumbersome preachment of a nihilistic text. Hundreds of workers and miles of fabric were mobilized to express the un-eventfulness of passage, and to depict time as a drone. As poets have realized, boundary walls are funny things. Boundary *films* which shut nothing out from nothing, and have an announced duration of two weeks – what are they but Trojan horses trying to punch a hole in the idea of shaping anything? Are the wonders of the world – the longest walls, tallest towers, most exquisite doorframes – essentially different from Christo's hoaxes, or basically the same? The largest monuments become, in this levelling view, kinds of anti-monument.

One of the wittiest negative monuments is the recreation of Franklin's house in Philadelphia by Robert Venturi, an empty *idea* of a building which is abnormally honest about the fact that none of the original survives and that we don't know what it was like. It is the

Christo's *Running Fence:* an anti-monument that took thousands of man-hours to make and lasted two weeks.

generalized outline of a house carried out in overscaled metal tubes painted hypothesis-grey. On the floors of the unroofed building are remarks inscribed in slate which passed between the garrulous Franklin and his wife on the various rooms while the house was going up.

It is a fabulous irony that *he wasn't there* and could only give generalized ideas of how he'd like it to be, or imagine dimly how it was turning out from her descriptions. For such a writing-man a verbal monument is most apt, but the visitor might slip into thinking that the disappearance of Franklin's house is a powerful negative sign, expressing the great *lack* of care that calmly let it disappear, only wishing for it back when it was too late.

And strangely enough the memorial leaves devastation in its wake – spaces all round it were cleared to be planted with Williamsburg-style gardens creating a lovely eighteenth-century calm, which was never there in Franklin's time, when it was densely built, a system of insalubrious courts. Venturi's memorial is by turns subtle and garrulous. Attached to the site by umbilical cords of underground ramps made more endless to accommodate the disabled, is a sizable museum concealed in the ground and containing little actual antiquity, being

Benjamin Franklin's house, Philadelphia, a reconstruction by Robert Venturi which acknowledges the fact that nothing of the original exists and no one knows what it looked like.

mostly loud-spoken advertisements of Franklin's greatness, the centre-piece of which was broken the day I went.

A history of house-memorials to great men would be an interesting thing to have. An earlier style was to coat the humble original in the most precious materials one could afford. This is more or less what's happened in Assisi where the church-memorial to Francis containing many works of the highest spiritual power is yet a perversion of his teaching, because it is complicated and magnificent and thus creates a partly social awe.

With real good will among their motives, his followers quickly set about marking off for special veneration the main scenes of his activity, so that today one can follow at second hand in accelerated form his steps, passing through turnstiles at many points along the way and feeling human scale swamped by institutions.

Francis has become a relic insulated by its containers from direct approach like the bells and wooden staffs of Irish saints, which were given tight fitting clothing of more expensive metal covered with interlace after the poor saint's death. And not only Francis but his follower Clare is now preserved in a horrible shrine where her sackcloth is displayed and explained by prisoner-nuns behind massive bars straight from a Gothic novel, and where her grave is circled by gaudy Victorian tunnels like the work of overambitious insects, and the remains and the grave they issued from have been turned into two different sensational sights on two different levels.

It is again piety which defaces its object, which has turned the humble rooms of Catherine of Siena into a glitter of sanctuary following illogically on sanctuary, at the top or bottom of another flight of stairs and keeping only in such spatial relation the memory that they once formed part of an ordinary dwelling, before acquiring their strange coating of ideal painted versions of the events which happened right here, or to these rooms' inhabitant when she went to Rome or Avignon. By now of course the canvases are valued as sixteenth-century works, good examples of a certain style, rather than as authoritative transcriptions of the saint's experience.

Perhaps viewers always neatly divide into those who look at the crucifix which spoke to Francis, or the one which gave Catherine five burning wounds, and suffer with the saint, and those who think 'oh a lovely example of thirteenth-century Tuscan painting.' In house-memorials maybe one can separate association-mongers from connoisseurs, at a glance, by the manner of their looking. But then again perhaps not. Perhaps real aesthetes despise shrines to great men because one can't always cordon off the aesthetic component of one's response.

Strangely enough the study or studio of someone we do not read or admire can be just as suggestive as the scene in which works we value were produced, as if we only need the idea of *someone* writing, to be set off on thoughts about long solitary bouts of thinking. Though it is not an easy thing actually to *see* with one's eyes, what one would really like to know is, how insufficient all the gathered mementoes seem to the *collector*, as an evocation of the missing hero.

In these places it would presumably be the most embarrassing lapse of decorum to have the subject and his family represented by waxwork replicas. For this is the heartland of ambiental values, where the Romantic theory that you colour your surroundings and they colour you enjoys maximum force. Is one justified in making a great divide between this branch of landscape theory – the object and the setting not two things but a continuum – and the relic-monger's feeling that there is power in the departed saint's leavings? Many observers have found the whole thing experimental for centuries – *will* these relics work (cure this ill, evoke this genius)? To know we must try them.

Monuments are not usually regarded as experimental. Most of them appear to know what they are talking about better than Franklin's House in Philadelphia. Yet perhaps some are more conjectural than they are taken to be, the erectors trying to impose a new idea of greatness, or wondering themselves, 'Can we really see X as a hero?' There are obvious cases of special pleading, shrines to obscure Provençal poets in their home towns, which one discounts as if they had been placed there by the immediate family. Monuments to those one has never heard of – not a class it is easy to become fervently interested in. In an obscure place in Basilicata one cannot escape reference to the hometown poet, Orazio Flacco – his house is present in the 1930s' idea of a Roman house, he has his square and his lifeless statue, and our hotel was named for him.

Obscure places have their obscure celebrities was what we thought. A Latin poet whom no one reads anymore, who either gave his name to, or is called after, flaccidity. Only when we got home did we realize that Orazio's name is known to every literate person: he is Horace, a most un-flaccid writer, yet not a current one any more, being part of a culture which has in the last forty years slipped much further into the mist, so that he is well on the way to being Orazio a writer no one has heard of. And he is marooned somewhat by being a person around whom there have been various flurries of commemoration, now dated – a fusty Victorian one (the statue), a boastful Fascist one (the house). Otherwise, one can't tell how Orazio was remembered in his home, and there are lots of years unaccounted for.

Monuments to the unknown, the forgotten, and to the wicked whom one would prefer to forget. When Bartolomeo Colleoni died, he left money to have a statue of *himself* erected in the main square at Venice. Apparently unable to throw out the request altogether, the rulers of Venice decreed that the statue be placed in the second-best square, which, such is the organization of the city, many fewer foreigners ever see, which is a many-times less eminent and notorious place than the vicinity of St Mark's. Having demoted the warlord, they engaged a sculptor who produced a monument which created awe. Taking away with one hand, they restored with the other. Now Colleoni (*Verrocchio*'s Colleoni) is a familiar figure, but seen more often between the pages of books than in the square of Zanipolo, being an obligatory stop on the pilgrimage through art history, if less so of Venice. The trouble for venerators of his memory is that it is as if his name was lost, and he were some Greek warrior dug up in a field without a history attached. But the point is to *survive* in bronze, not to be understood or appreciated, Colleoni would reply.

Monuments which seem to take the human figure as the measure of all things often make an intimidation of him, by showing him up on a high base with arm raised. An extended arm is surprisingly frequent in

Monument to the Russian
people's victory at Stalingrad
(now Volgograd), a figure
which seems at the same time
to glorify and to terrorize.

statues trying to impress us, and it is usually threatening. The huge
figure in the memorial at Stalingrad (now Volgograd) represents Russia
(i.e. us, not alien military might) but terrorizes none the less the tiny
people who creep round her base hoping not to wake her.

The statue of Liberty in New York harbour has had more than one
book written about her and become an institution which calls forth its
own commemorations. The ceremony marking its refurbishing must
have outdone the initial unveiling. But to an unprejudiced observer
Liberty's gesture is not so inevitably consoling. A warning it might be –
'Go back!' or a plea 'We can't see here. Bring light.' Liberty
Enlightening the World, the full title, is impossibly unrealistic. A much
better sculpture than it would have trouble being so comprehensive.

But to ask that Bartholdi impart some local truth or connection to his
work is completely to redraw the problem. However successfully, he is
talking about a quality not a person, not anything even so located as
'Russia'. Appropriately, like some ancient colossus, it is set astride water,
to be seen by those who've not yet landed, who are presently dislocated

Bartholdi's Statue of Liberty was erected in Montmartre, Paris, before being shipped to New York.

and unattached, or, more frequently, by those at her back, who know that her gesture is not really for them. It was a gift with strings attached which pulled it back toward its point of origin. It had been assembled and taken apart again in the streets of Paris, and the most astonishing views show it looming over the rooftops of Montparnasse, dwarfing a hill as it will later in some fashion a continent.

A kind of speech we are not capable of, except that the Gargantua-ism which is the strongest binding thread in American painting since the war might tempt one to other conclusions, though the inspiring content of most of these works is more opaque even than Bartholdi's. An artist whose imagination is more concrete than most, Claes Oldenburg, makes colossi which are both impersonal and highly dramatic, the detritus of persons. His giant popsicle melting between two rows of buildings like an inverted skyscraper in despondent mood, only fails to block the traffic entirely because a bite had been taken from it before it slipped from some giant child's hand, the bite leaving a ragged hole through which cars can be rerouted.

Claes Oldenburg's giant upside-down ice-lolly, proposed for Park Avenue, New York, is a comic parody of the over-scaled monument.

It memorializes a messy accident, the kind of thing which *does* happen in the street; it makes memorable an event which is better forgotten, and is ephemeral under normal conditions. If no steps are taken, the popsicle will be trodden into the pavement in a matter of hours and there will be nothing but a stain. Now the fiend-artist appears and makes our attention fix on an enlarged prolongation of such experience, which if we can banish ideas of stickiness and surfeit (these always too sweet, this big one too too sweet) we must admit has some of the qualities of Stonehenge.

Your ordinary monuments are decorations not obstructions. If they got in the way of new traffic schemes, in America they would be relocated. It is inconceivable that Americans would put up with old city gates which act on traffic flow like road repairs, squeezing it to one lane. Maybe that isn't the secret, European origin of Oldenburg's idea, but he is inventing a world in which we suffer our monuments, which will mean more if they are inconvenient and engage thus with the rest of life rather than standing apart from it.

He is also a Mannerist-doubler of meanings: the monument he devised for Toronto during air approaches to it, is upside down like the popsicle, a drain draining into Lake Ontario. Its water must have come from somewhere – the drain pipe is an explanation of origins. This lake is the collected waste of the city (at the time he designed it Ontario was one of the world's most heavily polluted). It is also a T for Toronto, and contains ski jumps and water slides which turn the journey of waste into enjoyable leisure. Like the Statue of Liberty it would end more as the city's joke on itself than as Oldenburg's condescension, an eminence, unlike most of them, which did not intimidate.

One thing has been left out. Oldenburg never imagined most of these monumental ideas would be built. Not that he wouldn't like to build them, but he has made it almost insuperably hard. They are useless like all the best monuments (Admiralty Arch in London loses status by including offices), they are possibly beyond present technical capacity, and they would be ruinously expensive. Most important, perhaps, they are affronts to the dignity and propriety that monuments embody.

One of the most flagrant or offensive of these is the monument proposed for London, which consists of two enormous toilet floats bobbing in the Thames. There are two, attached by long arms to Westminster Bridge, to obey the great artistic rule of symmetry, not any law in the construction of toilets. This takes its start from the fact the

Opposite: another freak of
Oldenburg's imagination,
*Proposed Colossal Monument
for Thames River: Thames
Ball* – two vast ballcocks or
toilet floats.
Left: the heads of presidents
Washington, Jefferson,
Teddy Roosevelt and
Lincoln carved in the cliffs of
Mount Rushmore, South
Dakota.

Thames is tidal and very dirty, so the ebb and flow works imperfectly like flushing. The monument is an unexpectedly expansive idea, not destructive. In some literal sense it defaces not London but a little square of cardboard, for it is drawn on a postcard of Parliament and the river, one of those lame boasts of which every city is the object. The fact is, Oldenburg pipes up, that the Thames is a rather horrible sight, not the blue mirror of the tinted photo.

Of all oversized monuments one of the most peculiar is the four heads jammed together on the cliff-face at Mount Rushmore, the only cultural feature for miles around, so why so uncomfortably crowded? The answer is partly that the rock gave way causing two of the faces to retreat into awkward corners the sculptor had never intended. One may forgive him his bad luck, but how can one continue to regard the grotesque result as an ideal fulfillment? In spite of the saga of his struggle for funds and recognition it is pretty disingenuous. Gutzon Borglum and not American virtue is principally advertised by this largest of garden gnomes or of billboards, planting the flag of civilization in another new spot where it does not really need to be.

Giant heads are in danger of looking decapitated, but it is an obvious way of suggesting, indelicately, superhuman scale. Obelisks, another sort of stand-in for an individual, show him as a semi-abstract integer, or more concretely, as a less characterful part of the body, an index finger or phallus. Mussolini's monolith in his new forum in Rome was one of the most elegant and reticent of such depictions of assertive selfhood.

The Washington Monument enjoys a complicated allegorical position in the grand scheme of Washington, a pivot which links the main institutions of this city named for him, to suggest his essential role in making executive and legislative, city and river, Maryland and Virginia form a harmonious whole. Except that oversight or malice entered the design, and this sharp point which forms a triangle with Capitol and White House was placed askew, so there is no right angle and the north–south axis is destroyed. It has its thus-sullied significance in the diagram of American government, and it also conveys or doesn't some notion of the general's character, whose guiding quality may be extrapolated as strength, blank stupidity or monomaniacal obsession.

The relation between a tower and what it symbolizes can be more obscure than this. The Eiffel Tower is the skeleton of a tower, further abstraction of an idea pretty skeletal to begin with. It has come to symbolize Paris, but in what way? For it was of course regarded as an eyesore at first, and as something which would be taken down. Like a mountain it is a symbol just because it is there.

Looking down on the Walter Scott Memorial in Edinburgh by G. Meikle Kemp, 1840–44.

Project for a Palace of the Soviets, topped by a giant statue of Lenin, to be built in the centre of Moscow, 1934.

The monument to Walter Scott in Edinburgh is a more lacy and picturesque version of this same idea, not quite a tower, rather a spire planted on the ground with a minimal shelter or enclosure under it. The appropriateness of Gothic is rather far fetched: he wrote books with medieval settings, but more important he gave the Scots their past, made it flesh, so a combination of temple and spire seemed right.

Lenin was to have had something similar if the plans had not bogged down in the swampy ground beside the Moscow River. The winning design for a Palace of the Soviets (how can workers' impromptu bodies want a palace? unless power itself is almost inevitably monarchical) shows a colossus on top of a column, a column so large it is one of the world's biggest skyscrapers. By this hybrid the Empire State Building and all other human constructions would be surpassed. In fact the design was revised and the figure of Lenin grew in order to keep up with the latest American office building. But how would this process have been carried on once it was actually built?

It would have contained amazing things. The gigantic pedestal of this 270-foot icon was to be full of huge meeting halls, where under the image of Lenin orating, speeches would actually be uttered. But to call

Endless Column by Constantin Brancusi, made of cast iron in 1937 for a public park in Romania.

these real functions in this setting is perhaps naive, for they would have been largely ceremonial, and the crowds at these meetings would have formed a kind of dumb monument.

The building progressed past the postcard stage, but slowly, it was so overblown. In one year just before the war its foundations gobbled up 17 per cent of the national steel production, an example of a people nearly killing itself to symbolize something.

New York is either the most or the least symbolic of cities. Seen from far enough away, from Russia for example, it appears nothing but a collection of memorial columns, memorials to something more ineffable surely than commercial triumphs. Rockefeller Center is a high-minded translation of the fetish of height into civic amenity and would probably prove a revealing object of social study.

But the most metaphysical of all such efforts is Brancusi's Endless Column, a joke on the concept which is trying not to be one, which reverses the normal order of flow. Ordinarily they do not grow upward but thrust downward. First you have a column (these appeared in Rome) which instead of holding a roof up, marks a spot or an event, an independent entity freed from structural responsibility. And then eventually you get Brancusi's which doesn't even terminate but goes on and on like a plant, forming the most awkward art-object in the world, defying gravity and death.

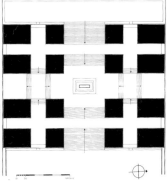

Monument to the Missing of the
Somme, at Thiepval, northern
France, by Lutyens, 1924 and
(*above*) its plan.

Triumphal arches by themselves contain the seeds of paradox, for
they are another structural element pried loose from working structure.
They soon come to seem a perversion of that means of making openings
or entrances in walls. Lutyens analyzed the form remorselessly, and in
the war memorial at Thiepval in Picardy made a construction of
interlocked arches like a pile of them, which seems to multiply
hollowness.

They are always buildings over as soon as they have begun, originally
stages on a ceremonial route which gave the hero a chance to enter the
city prostrate at his feet over and over again, a process grotesquely
pompous and fictional in a way only a distended empire could swallow.
The *plan* of Lutyens' arch makes clearer why it expresses so well the
imposing pointlessness of all those English deaths in France. It is like a
complicated criss-cross sum which totals zero.

Even more abruptly than Lutyens, Brancusi reduces the strutting and
inflation of a thousand memorial arches to laughter. His Kissing Gate is
another joke on pomposity. Arches 'kiss', coming from two sides to
meet over a void and stay stuck together. Brancusi's form kisses and
facilitates kissers (a person can just fit under). Its lintel is held up by four
couples each making an abstract form like glued lips.

This sculptor gives the famous muteness of monuments an erotic
cause. At the other end of the scale are the memorials which are born

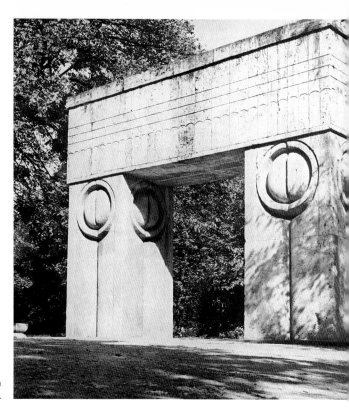

Kissing Gate by Brancusi,
1937, in the same Romanian
park as the Endless Column.

with speeches in their mouths, a whole class of hortatory monument,
which attempts to stir the viewer with slogans and inscriptions, least
subtle but to some human faculty the most satisfying monuments of all.
For we like to see things spelled out, nothing omitted. One of the most
moving monuments in America consists of two black slabs like the half-
buried pages of a huge book displaying nothing but 500,000 finely
carved names. So described, it sounds about as interesting as the
telephone directory. In fact it is one of the most nearly adequate war
memorials which exists, and its immense popularity convinces one that
monuments can sometimes perform great healing functions in society.

The Vietnam memorial is another cover-up of this much lied-about
conflict; seen from behind, the monument is buried or entombed: it
hardly breaks the surface. But this unemphatic presence has unexpected
power to draw people into it like an open, still seething wound, a rent in
the surface which focuses one's attention compulsively. Standing
behind it where no one comes because nothing is there, one sees two
orderly files of visitors disappearing beneath the ground like an episode
from Dante. Standing in front of the pages, one becomes part of those
coming or those going, or stops to trace a name with one's hand like one

of the blind, or to frame a particular name in the aperture of one's camera, impossible task without markers which the monument won't provide.

It expresses the enormity of the event by the tininess of each barely legible victim, lost in an oceanic wash of thousands. The memorial constructs difficulties for itself and for us – those lost are arranged not alphabetically but chronologically, in the order they fell, or is it in the order that the news reached us, in what central place would that be? So there must be keepers of other books nearby which alphabetize the names, and these are exactly like telephone directories and lead one to a numbered column. As a filing system it reminds me of an old-fashioned library which shelves its books according to when it received them.

And there are further imposed intricacies. The list begins on the right hand of these two wedge-shaped pages, starting big and growing smaller until, vanishing at one end, it restarts as a sliver again at the other. Does this doubling back express some uncertainty or complexity of feeling? Soldiers lost in the same month are at opposite ends of this strange universe of letters.

How would it feel as one of the missing (they are included too) to

The Vietnam memorial in Washington. The surface which looks like a mirror is in fact polished black stone bearing 500,000 names of those killed and missing in the Vietnam war.

return and trace one's name here? Perhaps not so unsettling as we imagine. It isn't exactly like being plastered on a hoarding in Times Square. The names are in some sense illegible because there are so many in such a small space, though continually washed and freshened by the generalized attention lavished on them. It is rare among monuments in creating an *activity* – not aimless gaping or directionless wandering – which is more forceful than itself.

But perhaps this Dantean vividness was not foreseen by the monument's deviser. The directories do not look as if they formed part of the original plan. Maybe no one anticipated that the list would be animated this way, because people arrived wanting to look something up. Although no one is buried there, the Vietnam memorial is like one ideal of the cemetery maker, where the dead are not left to moulder indistinguishably but are picked out and become the focus of individual attention. A large enough collection of monuments usually becomes a crowded city in which no one stands out, or a few are seized at random by the viewer's whim.

At some point the nature of the Vietnam memorial will change, as the event it commemorates becomes less embarrassing and as survivors disappear who remember the people whose names it is made of. At some point, it too will become inert, commemorating something truly forgotten, except by historians or the historian in us. While the memory is raw, this monument stirs it more tellingly than anyone could have predicted. Perhaps afterward an answering process will take its place, and this anti-monument will seem so enigmatic it needs explaining, and then it will stay notorious because in the white and pompous city it is black and inconspicuous.

CHAPTER III

Fortification, Ideal Cities

THE ACT of monumentalizing fortifications, seeing them as oversized sculptural forms, is part of the aftermath of use. Even one's own defences, while actually functioning or believed capable of function, will not always seem utterly benign. There must have been sensitive medieval souls who entered the town walls many times to visions of slaughter like those that most of us would experience passing missile silos today, if we knew where they were. But now almost all architecturally potent fortifications are so long outmoded that we don't even bother to establish the sequence of obsolescence, like not knowing whether a 1930s or 50s automobile is newer.

These formerly threatening objects have become curiosities of which one makes tours, not because human aggression has dried up, though perhaps in selected places certain forms of it have – Tuscan cities don't fear yearly invasion by marauding private armies. Nowadays no one can quite come out with theories like Ruskin's that war is good for society, but in almost all popular accounts of medieval and early modern history flow strong undercurrents of envy at the energy of medieval Italians, of which the surest proof is frequent little wars.

So the modern interest in massive obsolete defences is maybe not purely formal. And when one considers that Michelangelo was called in to design fortifications for Florence, or looks at the distinctive two-toned banding of Caernarfon Castle, one is less sure that the old approach was always purely functional. Not that such purity of purpose is as feasible as might be supposed, but one can tell looking at many factories that they have no thought of being looked at, and behave in some fashion as if they weren't there. Whereas the castles associated with towns, or around which towns have grown up, are bits of conscious display.

Admittedly the Edwardian castles of Wales (of which Caernarfon is one, and Rhuddlan, Conwy, and Beaumaris the most interesting others) are very special instances. Like Wren's city churches they form a connected set whose designers take care (as in the production of

Caernarfon Castle, North Wales. Polygonal towers and polychrome banding are features more aesthetic than military.

snowflakes) not to repeat themselves while making another of this recognizable type, which is partly their own invention, partly well established tradition. Not many of the original Welsh inhabitants could have made a tour of these castles, appreciating the ingenious variations on a small number of themes – angularity, plumpness, clustering – but clearly *someone* was meant to. Perhaps it was imagined this would be done sitting in London perusing the jewel-like plans, even superimposing them on each other, more often than slogging through Wales. Even to this day it isn't easy to find all the plans collected together like snowflakes, yet to see them that way must be counted the greatest pleasure offered by the project.

The associated towns have multiplied many times in size in succeeding centuries but are still dominated by the castles. So is Welsh architectural history. It may be one of the charms of Wales that the national temperament is so ungrandiose it has never got in the habit of real architecture (as opposed to dwellings, sheds, and small meeting rooms) but it remains a galling embarrassment that many of the proudest structures in the country are English.

One can feel satisfaction that these monuments imposed on Wales are now wrecks, yet this is a two-edged fact. Walking under the walls of Caernarfon Castle, one is most divertingly oppressed. Instead of the

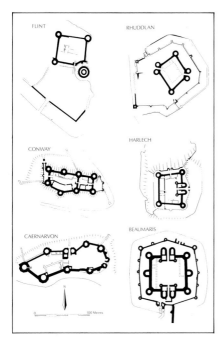
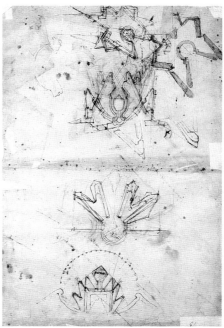

Fortifications as an art-form. *Left:* plans of six Welsh castles built under Edward III. *Right:* sketches for fortifications in Florence by Michelangelo.

usual round lumps of stone punctuating unscalable cliffs of wall, one has even more broken forms at the pivots. Each tower is pointed like the prow of a ship, making a whole which is thorny like a giant sea urchin and in spite of its ample dimensions similarly ticklish to contain or cohabit with.

But the coloured banding built so firmly into the fabric of this castle sets it off even more than its crystalline shape. For it shows a kind of premeditation we assume defensive necessities do not allow. It is foppish or precious, a fort's equivalent of dressing up, to arrange the two different colours of huge blocks in irregular bands as if it were all a kind of inlay. So along with stylized brittleness of form goes the nearest thing to a decorative treatment of the surface one can find in a functioning castle of so early a date.

In 1528 Michelangelo was engaged to design up-to-date batteries and gates for the already existing fortifications surrounding Florence, which now lay under threat from invading French armies. In the event, none of them appear to have been built, whether because events moved too fast and the French armies had swept over Florence before there was time, or because the value of his proposals was doubted.

But they remain in impressive drawings, which show him spurred by these ugly necessities to produce a strange new vertebrate anatomy,

69

clearly descended from his skeletal and muscular studies. At other times a gateway seen in plan resembles standard types of Mannerist ornament (originally arrived at by putting architectural forms through the distorting filter of the human body) bounded and kept in tension by a system of straight lines which are (it dawns on us) the lines of sight for firing at attackers. Threat has converted the simple idea of entry into a complex one, full of hesitations and second thoughts. Perhaps we enjoy most the comparison which is almost a pun, between one kind of organization and another, crystal and organism, a link the designer might not be very mindful about preserving when these actually came to be built.

The English Mannerist Thomas Tresham used far fetched analogies as protective disguises to keep his meaning from prying eyes. He was Catholic in a country paranoiacally suspicious of Catholics, and the normal version is that he was driven by necessity to encode his messages, not a natural but a circumstantial mannerist. So on the walls of his prison cell one found endless numerical calculations and apparently disjunctive letters of the alphabet, which signified to him various dates in Hebrew history or events in the life of Mary.

When he got out, his long hatched plans for intricate, useless, and in this special way defensive, structures could be carried out. He undertook three new buildings in his career, only one of which he brought to completion, the smallest and richest, though all three are small and rich. It is the most like an impregnable fort and the most functionless, or trivial in its apparent function.

Now known as the Triangular Lodge, it graced the grounds of his house at Rushton in Northamptonshire. Which is to say that its baffling messages wouldn't have reached many hostile eyes. This building designed by a man with 'three' in his name took three years to complete. It is three-sided (Father, Son, and Holy Ghost), three-storeyed, and variously three-d on each side – 3 gables, 3 rows of 3 windows, 3 steps to the door, 33 letters in each cornice inscription and plenty of ornamental trefoils and triangles (three trefoils were Tresham's arms).

Tresham found himself in the thrilling plight that to mention himself was also to mention God, a *T* was visible code for this Northampton landowner *and* for the Three-in-One who ruled the universe, like a T-square which measures off all creation and which also begins the English and Latin words for this name of God (Trinitas, Trinity). But in spite of its concentration of surface meaning, his little fort which looms vertiginously over the observer, so exaggerated is its height in relation to other dimensions, is a hoax or dead sea fruit. Essentially it is pure sign

Thomas Tresham's Triangular Lodge, Rushton, Northamptonshire, where a rabbit-keeper lived among abstruse theological meanings.

and contains nothing; the only use he could think of for it was lodging the keeper of his rabbits.

So it is one of the first garden eye-catchers, a bit of obscurity which one expects to find guarding something precious, but is mostly expended in its external aspect. Like a fortress it has its end in the wall which baffles or repels. Once breached it reverts from the strongest to the weakest of buildings.

The history of fortification must be fuller than most of such paradox. The advent of new offensive weapons has many times thrown constructors of defences into convulsion. Metal bullets and explosive mines, both of which appeared late in the fifteenth century, caused powerful regression in the architectural form of defences. Suddenly high walls looked more vulnerable, and no base could be too thick or stable, so you get constructions like Salses, built by the Spanish in Rousillion, lone survivor of a considerable group.

At Salses the crystalline geometry of late medieval castles has been blurred back into the landscape by the addition of extensive skirts and swathings of masonry, as if one had begun with a clear star-figure and by successive coatings reduced it to a vaguer lump. The result somewhat

Right: Salses, Rousillon, a medieval castle-plan thickened and blurred by the need to withstand artillery.
Far right: Berkamsted, Hertfordshire, a Norman castle of the motte-and-bailey type. The motte is the castle mound, the bailey the walled enclosure.

resembles primitive motte-and-baileys of Romanesque times made of earth mounded up on the far side of the ditch which their substance came out of. Sometimes these survive, as at Berkhamsted, without the later timber and then masonry improvements from the days when teetery towers on top of pointed mounds were actually enhancements of strength.

The resemblance between sophisticated Salses and humble Berkhamsted is thus somewhat delusive. Berkhamsted is only beginning to aspire to definite shapes of masonry, while Salses is being driven back into the earth, putting heavy protective muffles on its beautiful forms.

To us, Berkhamsted is a mildly artificial bit of landscape, manmade hills and valleys abrupt enough for us to want to climb them. However much we may fancy that Salses is reverting to buried forms or becoming geological, no one needs to tell us what it is. But without explanatory notices one would probably not guess that the humps at Berkhamsted preceded and gave impetus to the settlement.

For a number of reasons prehistoric hill-forts are even more imperceptible. Though one has doubts whether they are there at all, they are the most impressive of all, for they *are* the promontories, works

in which the site is the building. True, there are a few dishevelled piles of stones, even a 'wall' following a circuit as unfocused as a contour line on a map. But it is usually so collapsed it would hardly keep out a sheep. If one is no expert one looks at stone teeth poking out of the ground in decayed rows and wonders whether they are a fiendish kind of early tank trap or a natural outcropping.

Maybe such guesses are nearer a part of the truth than archaeologists' theories. Though one needed them to find one's way here in the first place. In prehistoric times the distinction between buildings and outcroppings wasn't what it is for us. You built on outcroppings, and you didn't add enough to cause fundamental alteration in their shape.

The function and history of such 'constructions' or sites is so obscure that this darkness is the main appeal to many observers. The history of almost any later defensive establishment is loaded with the kind of irony we have been told is the discovery of the nuclear age. Expensive weapons systems which were never used or grew obsolete before being tested in combat, the history of warfare and especially of fortification is littered with them. Defences which were never tested may have served their purpose, proving thus effective deterrent to attackers, or have shown by this their complete irrelevance.

73

Very few forts and castles' history give solid comfort to believers in the idea of them. Salses, at least, did not remain, like the marvellous defences of Berwick-on-Tweed, Lucca, or Naarden, purely a spectacle which no one ever actually challenged. Salses was attacked four times – in 1503, twice in 1639, finally in 1642. After the last it escaped razing by a hairsbreadth, probably because the cost was prohibitive.

Its performance wasn't particularly magnificent. The walls were breached almost at once in 1503, and the Spanish only saved the day by tunnelling outside and blowing up a number of themselves along with several hundred French. Accounts of the next siege read like speculations about the end of Mayan civilization. Did the French breach the wall (no sign of this survives) or did a traitor let them in? Later in the same summer the Spanish recaptured it.

Static defences function ambivalently, and this must influence the way we see them. They are traps, but for whom? Those whom they pull toward them and keep in place outside the walls? Or those they expose while seeming to protect, who soon find supplies running short and realize there is more to safety than having a shield between yourself and a ring of attackers? One must always hesitate to build too well, foreseeing one's work fallen into the enemy's hands, but perhaps one takes comfort in the fact that a common aftermath to the capture of a fort is its deliberate destruction.

The small fortified houses of Scotland at first seem a revealing graph of a society which wore its violence outwardly until much later than almost any English place. Records of how useful these defences were seem hard to come by, and looking at the larger ones we usually find traces of antiquarianism. Against the original towers have been built some not very defensible but comfortable rooms. So the whole complex, with lower wings linking forbidding towers, is a compact summary of troubled history, and an ideal version of Scottish character, more rugged and more relaxed than Southern ones. So even if the effective cause of the towers' survival is reluctance to tear down anything well built however obsolete, the result now is a species of building which bridges nature and culture in a way even cave dwellings can't, because they lack this sense of transition.

In certain parts of Scotland one comes across fortified churches as one does in southwestern France. To us it is an impossible contradiction and sends us looking for signs of religious conflict, not just an unsettled political climate. We assume that this form would never have been hit on until the building's predecessor or another nearby had been flattened in a raid; it only makes sense as the fruit of bitter experience.

Drum, Aberdeenshire, an early Scottish fortified house with later, less defensible, rooms built against it.

Between this stage and the mimicry in late Gothic churches of battlements around the top of castle walls one imagines no connection at all, a positive hiatus in the memory. The battlement seems by this point not even a metaphor, but simply an image, wanting to extract the aesthetic benefits of a toothed silhouette and no more, encouraging the view that architectural form is finally decorative and not symbolic, and hinting the style is not long for this world.

Against this frivolity or formalism one can set a peculiar nineteenth-century castle mimicry. Prisons had already been granted their special stylistic codes (Dance's Newgate in super-rustication the best of them) before the first one turned up with towers, portcullis and machicolation. This was the model which caught on however, as if one knew at a glance that's what a prison should look like. On the Eastern Penitentiary of 1823–36, at Philadelphia, as presumably elsewhere, it was only façadism. Internal walls weren't Cyclopean or grotesquely thick, and primitive services were cost-cutting measures not historical reminiscences.

The better it was done the more terrifying this symbolism could be. When H.H. Richardson came to design an insane asylum for Buffalo he made it an impregnable fort in gloomy purple masonry capped by cold

Buffalo State Hospital, USA, by H.H. Richardson, an asylum for the insane with suggestions of castle or prison.

green roofs. The joke or appropriateness of using castle to mean prison was that so many castles had in the end spent more time keeping prisoners in than attackers out.

Nineteenth-century castle-prisons (and castle-asylum) didn't signal a return to medieval methods of treatment, not exactly, but they wouldn't encourage anyone (keeper, inmate, or passerby) to think that society hoped the criminal would become good or the madman get well. Who can calculate how many were driven further from sanity by the sight of the Buffalo asylum looming over them like an apparition in a Gothic tale? How far would one trust the warder who indulged in such weird excesses?

Here is a symbolism with noxiously divisive effect; we think there are others which are more like innocent fakery. In Elizabethan England great houses are near enough to the need to be fortified for their reminiscences to carry a kind of conviction. They have not gone far afield for ways of being impressive or gloomy, but taken the nearest to hand, not so much a historical excursion as a hangover from the past. Now we notice the way in which these houses are Gothic, but to contemporaries it must have been more striking that they departed so boldly from earlier custom.

From certain aspects Burghley, one of the biggest prodigy houses, looks like a fort with lots of holes punched in it. One can't help feeling

Wollaton, in Nottinghamshire, is a Jacobean house pretending to be a castle in some medieval romance.

that this paradox is gleefully exploited – the landowner builds powerful walls and then he demolishes them by the insertion of windows. Of course one doesn't really have the walls, and then the windows, but there were enough examples of modernizing dreary old piles by letting in the light for this illusion to gain ground.

Others go further than Burghley – Wollaton and then Hardwick – but the effect is already as if the window gives the pattern to the entire fabric. As a window is a web of slender members lending stiffness to a transparent film or membrane, so the whole wall becomes now 'mullions' and 'transomes' running between 'panes' which are the large windows. Thus the building is dematerialized, becoming a glittering figment like the spider's web.

Surely all that brittle angularity is not on the point of vanishing? Yet one notes features like the repeated corner towers at Wollaton, of unimaginable but monotonous complexity, the most imposing part of the building become *all* ornament, at least in its upper reaches, the first to be damaged in an attack but the easiest to repair. All this piercing and furling is, then, a fantastic rendition of ruined or broached towers. And the style has become so willful and confident that it hardens into flimsiness in the least expected places.

Towers, from being the meat of the building have become the dessert, vehicles of senseless display. At Hardwick it is hard to count them, because they fall into such confusing zig-zag patterns, yet at the same time appear detached as if the entire structure were only a group of upward thrusts. Some of the most wonderful Elizabethan façades, even small ones (such as Fountains Hall in the West Riding), play with symmetrical looming eminences like a whole city skyline.

Most fanciful or wholehearted of all is the so called Little Castle at Bolsover in Derbyshire. The whole complex includes several distinct sets of building, which one assumes belong to different periods and conceptions of castle life. First the Little Castle set apart and half surrounded by an older wall, with its own guard house and defences, then the long Terrace Range like a home-made royal palace, and attached to it the Riding School, another bit of paraphernalia one associates with courts.

Great one's surprise on finding that the antiquated Little Castle which turns the medieval curtain into a garden wall, with seats and pavilions hidden in its thickness, and a pleasure walk along its top, that this cranky but soundly based bit of make-believe is almost exactly contemporary with the extroverted terrace range. Building went forward on both at once. The Castle from the start was a playhouse, for theatrical banquets, jousts, masques – medieval revivals which took place within sight of a modern gentleman's dwelling.

The nineteenth and twentieth centuries can imagine resurrecting castles, but not in sight of a later habitation. William Burges at Castell Coch lost himself in reinstating all the machinery of an old castle in working order. The obsolete devices are so long disused that to see missing, perhaps even unsuspected, parts replaced gives the whole a newfangledness which makes the restorer seem inventor.

Appropriately the last real English castle ever built outdid Burges in hubris and eccentric costliness, cloaking this in barbaric plainness instead of Burges' colourful luxury. Julius Drew (later Drewe), the builder of Castle Drogo in Devon, began by finding himself a Norman ancestor (Drogo, or Dru), then a village named after him, Drewsteignton, then a suitable site nearby for a castle, though no one pretended the ground had ever held one. Here the fiction may have been expected to break, but it didn't, at least not at once. Drewe obtained the enthusiastic connivance of the best architect of the age, Edwin Lutyens, and they set about concocting the most preposterous bit of functioning stage scenery privately built in this century. It was to have granite walls six feet thick, a specification which made even Drewe, in sole command of an enormous fortune he'd made from scratch in fifteen years as a tea trader, reduce the original extent of the whole project. Both architect and client

The 'Little Castle' of Bolsover, Derbyshire, another make-believe castle built as a setting for jousts and masques.

for their different reasons had a consuming enthusiasm for granite, and Lutyens had to dissuade Drewe from building in undressed blocks of gigantic size.

In the end, after twenty years of construction, with a war in the middle, he got an unnervingly sleek building, in an abstract sense Lutyens' most modern, because it is able to concentrate as few of his others can on pure wall and pure perforation of it. Since battlements make and are known by everyone to make no sense at all, they become pure angular expression, and Lutyens a kind of Cubist while pandering to reactionary ancestral fantasies.

Like some of Norman Shaw's wittiest buildings, the Castle inserts bogus historical scenarios: a learned detective could trace 'later' additions and refinements in its fabric, stairs plopped into spaces not planned for them, fancy moldings overlaid on a rude base (was this drawing room in some earlier age a dungeon?).

But ironies here catch up with everyone. Drewe died a year after moving into his new–old house. And Lutyens found himself most free in starved service corridors and kitchens buried so deep in the mass they

Castle Drogo, Lutyens' (and the 20th century's) last essay in the castle style, built before and after World War I.

could only be lit by skylights. The careful historical facsimile had, like a dinosaur revived from a swamp, a shorter life just *because* it was uncompromisingly true to outmoded scales. It fell into the hands of the National Trust forty-five years after first functioning as the ancestral home. Its life was over before it began, an imaginary past not a true future.

But this is apt. The service quarters, Burges-mechanisms of a century later, do not need to be wasted on servants and on use. Their abstract qualities are now savoured by every paying guest, an outcome perhaps not unhoped for by the architect. Whatever others may have thought Lutyens was not one to miss all the signs of England's decline. But he didn't cease to build large or confidently just because he saw hints that the commissioning society would fall away. The buildings would survive, making their claim on men's notice by different qualities. The pantries and larders at Drogo were never meant to blush unseen for long.

The Fascist style of grand construction often resembled a fortified building, not to signify that the party was unpopular and might be attacked, but to awe with insuperable strength long before questions

were asked. The problem in old Italian cities was where to put these
political advertisements, of which every considerable urbs should have
at least one. For the best places were already taken. Not that the Fascists
were averse to major remanagement, as they proved at Lecce, where
they had the excuse of classical (the preferred vintage) remains
underlying the medieval (less prestigious, less imperial) centre for their
project of uncovering and then partly rebuilding on a choice sector in
the city core. But there was a limit to the amount of tampering one
could do in prized spaces like the main square in Pistoia for example.
Various solutions were found: in Pistoia the party building survives in a
street just behind and below the square, with no direct line of sight into
it, jammed so near the façades opposite that its pomp is constrained. In
Arezzo the method is to apply a thin layer of Fascist colonnade along the
top side of an important T-shaped space in the centre. However
disruptive this may have seemed at the time, the present effect is discreet
if not quite timid: the planner acknowledged that there were limits to his
power; he could have only one of those surfaces which meet here, and he
could apply only a shallow coating to that. It wasn't a penetrating
presence.

An obvious alternative was to try and set up a countercentre at the
edge of the historic core. Sometimes this must have produced a
devastating sense of the irrelevance of Fascism. Or maybe officials didn't
sit there wondering, why does no one use *our* square? Maybe they rested
content with a Chirico vision: our monuments will survive humanity –
here they are already in a depopulated world.

Scenographically if not socially one of the most effective solutions
was to place the massive new palaces along a seafront boulevard, so that
instead of cramped streets they looked out on the infinite. In Taranto
and Bari this is where one will find the Fascist fortifications, conversing
with their equal the sea. But many users of these buildings must have
been struck by feelings of irrelevance, even if only in the few seconds it
took to walk round the mass backing onto the city fabric before one
reached the grand entrance giving onto nothing.

Today with their teeth pulled these piles are like Lutyens castles, pure
pomp without real weight. They are lavish, yet stern, bigger than one
expects, giving a strong sense of the undivided mass, with details which
are too big as well, as if an office building had four windows like a house,
but of a size commensurate with itself. No one would believe those huge
details! Rather, no one would *quite* believe them, and they'd have their
effect in changing expectations, as would happen if important people
began wearing monstrous epaulettes.

On the Prettura at Taranto are displayed enormous metal-looking fasces, enormous eagles, enormous railings, enormous letters relaying the obvious, or one of the simplest and cleverest Fascist tricks: ANNO XII. Renumbering is even more effective than the old totalitarian habit of renaming. How cheaply the government simplifies our lives. Like the buildings, it is a proclamation of self-belief which though improbable carries a certain force. Larger amounts of stone are harder to disbelieve, colossal errors harder to detect.

A successful attempt to block the view and surround the viewer with a blank world of masonry occurs at Carcassonne, where the most powerful experience is to get lost between the inner and outer rings of defences. This city is really the last word in town walls, because it has two concentric sets of them, with the unforeseen result that however sullied by tourism the captive town inside has now become, there is a free zone where nothing is built and virtually no one comes, where one can indulge one's historical fantasies to the full.

It isn't in the proprietors' interest to reveal to us how completely Carcassonne is a latter day fabrication. So Viollet-le-Duc's name is left off the careful diagram of the town's sixty-plus towers which is sold there. Instead, one finds the unexplained little announcement that 'The Cité of Carcassonne owes its conservation to J.P. Cros-Mayrevielle,' a classic case of the reassertion of local ownership. Cros-Mayrevielle was a native-born archeologue who devoted his life to publicizing Carcassonne. When he managed to attract Viollet-le-Duc that was the decisive step, for Viollet was the most persuasive revivalist in France. His interest in Carcassonne led to a sustained labour lasting thirty-five years, one of the largest archaeological reconstructions ever undertaken.

Recognizing the size of his opportunity, Viollet made Carcassonne a museum of the history of fortification. True, it had been gradually improved over a long span, with bursts of construction at several different periods, from Roman to early, middle, and late medieval. From this Viollet made the bizarre extrapolation that in its prime it would have retained pure examples from each stage of construction.

His greatest contribution is what draws the crowds, the skyline. But all those witches' hats are now known to be uncalled for, not native to the south of France, imported from harsher climes. The higher he went the more hypothetical he became, with a result inefficient from any view but the picturesque: no incident is one-too-many for someone whose job is simply to look.

Still, Viollet has performed an essential function. He has taken a hand in history, instead of accepting supinely what the past offers him. For all

Carcassonne, in southern France, survived with its double circle of walls intact. The tops and roofs are restorations.

its studious errors it is a high water mark of sympathetic entry into the alien – excessively literal minded, and inelegant in its pretended faithfulness to *every* past phase, but art is always literal, at least, and the past is even more of a mess than Viollet's controlled admissions allow.

The Elizabethan bastions of Berwick-on-Tweed are found in something much nearer the state of nature than Carcassonne, yet one often feels the pressure of the conserving hand, for there are many now-useless acres kept in limbo as teachers of precious historical lessons and no more. Here lesser traces of various earlier builds remain but have not been mocked up into a false equality with their replacements.

Like most grandiose plans, the sixteenth-century defences of this city were curtailed at various points and in the end left incomplete, with fatal gaps which would probably have spelled disaster if the city had ever been attacked. It was not, so the debates of the engineers have a pleasantly academic air. They could agree to jettison the northern part of the city, which had been included in the medieval walls, as presenting topographical difficulties. The prettiest plans show a six-pointed, star-like figure whose near-perfection depends on slicing off another sector, the district lying inconveniently lower to the south. But as this

contained the royal storehouses, it fought its way back inside the plan, giving a compromise result no one would have designed from scratch. The Italian expert called in had already been ignored, in part because his plans would have meant even làrger bills (and the unused defences of Berwick are already one of the largest public projects of Elizabeth's reign, without his walls running clear to the coast), perhaps in part because he was Italian. So, with vast expense and long pondering, Berwick got a sort of botch, half or two-thirds of a complete system of defences in a certain mode (soon to be obsolete even if it had been perfect). Work ceased because of a more immediate French threat somewhere else, and a sufficient quota of national attention was never focused here again.

All of which is neither here nor there to the tourist. The incomplete ramparts are still the best in England and let one grasp the astonishing scale, devilish intricacy, and final simple-mindedness in this stage of human self-outwitting. A large proportion of the visible masonry in these immense bastions – of which six were proposed and three (and parts of others) built – is thrown into 'flankers' tucked behind the ears of the arrowhead, which cover a blind spot left by the larger geometry and give one a clear line of fire over the last few yards before the wall. They plug a hole which should never have been there at all, and break down one's defence against a continuous charge into two disconnected segments.

Many ideal cities were projected or at least drawn during the Renaissance, but the nearest thing to a realization of the theories was a

Two towns dominated by their defences: Berwick-on-Tweed (*left*) – an air view and detail of one of the bastions to show the line of fire – and Palmanova, in Italy (*right*), the most perfect of the star-plans, a geometrical 'ideal city'.

Venetian military outpost, Palmanova – which is to say that the best practical excuse for such perfection was defence or fortification. In fact the history of such geometrizations of life prompts a suspicion of deeper accord between military purposes and cities planned from scratch than the purely practical one.

Defeated by the Turks the Venetians needed to drop back from the castle at Gradisce, so the new frontier would be a little kernel or showpiece of Venetian civilization which carried within it all urban functions in abbreviated form and not just the warmaking ones.

Like many plans of the preceding century which never got off the page, Palmanova is concentric, a nine-pointed star or snowflake which breaks into three's. Its three entrances and three roads-out form a Y-figure, the arms of which meet in a central square, which is an essence within a concentrate, to this day an idea unfulfilled, the emptiest place in Palmanova, where the city's very existence is called in question.

Presumably it should suit connoisseurs that the 'city' is still so largely an idea. Its streets have not filled with activity, its squares have not come into use. It still feels like a colonial outpost waiting for settlers to dispose themselves in the surrounding countryside and wake its functions into life. Perhaps ideal cities are doomed to remain uninhabited, or find themselves gradually submerged in life indistinguishable from life pure and simple, not ideal.

Palmanova is precious because it has never grown up to the original specifications. Although it is small (no more than 1200 metres across), as it turned out it was bigger than it needed to be. Even late in the nineteenth century the filling-out remained uneven, as if the clothes were not only too big but made provision for extra limbs the wearer didn't have. So one finds maps showing only the three main routes built up, and all the other symmetrical net of streets laid out, but lying entirely idle. In the original conception there had been a ring of subsidiary squares halfway to the edge, six of them, disposed in pairs between the main roads. It is a lovely idea, but it hasn't really thought about what makes or calls forth a square.

Rightly or not we assume that Italian squares are guardians of many secrets about civic life. One of the secrets is deficiency in central control. All kinds of infringements are tolerated, but probably such variety is just the current outcome of long jockeying between public and private forces.

No wonder then that planned squares of the sixteenth century, even though planned by Italians, feel nothing like Italian squares. In Palmanova public space is a kind of bounded vacancy, and the feeling extends into every corner of the plan. Wherever one is within it one is in the same place. The curve of the curved streets is always the same and the stiff rays come at predictable intervals according to how far from the hub one has strayed. So one keeps absolute track of where one is, yet every position is completely uncharacterized, and one has a sinister sense of being watched, as if such geometric control is an attempt to oversee one's movements. Strangers can't get comfortable here except in the central hollow, which in its turn seems to propel one down one of the exit tubes.

The roads out reveal another ramification of pure ideality. These three equidistant rays are labelled with destinations – Udine, Cividale, Aquileia, as if the whole landscape is organized on the stellar or crystalline pattern, empty except for an evenly spaced web of other nodes, like a black night lit up by occasional points of brightness. The three roads fan out, all oblique to the Turkish threat in the East: thus the compass point which controls the whole idea is not acknowledged by the plan. If one looks at the map one finds that although these three towns are equidistant from Palma, not one is really in the specified direction, and they form a crooked triangle in which Palma lies off to the side, not comfortably in the middle.

The world is not like that, we retort to the planners – yet why shouldn't the pretence be maintained? Military commanders need accurate maps, but the ordinary traveller (as long as he sticks to main roads) will suffer no inconvenience from his belief that the whole landscape arranges itself regularly in a pattern of stars, and he may never

Mississauga, Canada, is an artificial town created as an administrative centre and given its identity by its city hall.

perceive, seeing everything at eye level and not from the zenith, that the road to Udine takes him north and not toward the ideal northwest that the Palma-diagrams show.

The inventor or institutor of true ideal cities must be good at ignoring the evidence of his senses and at seeing what isn't there. The most powerful ideal cities are the most unlikely, not idealizations of something which already exists, or magisterial improvements like the squares of Paris and London, but ordinations in places or conditions where one would have said a city could not come.

Intellectually one of the boldest architectural ventures of the present is the new city hall for a non-place in Canada on the outskirts of Toronto. Outskirts are in some way the most unlikely spot to create centres or eminences, and Mississauga, the town which will be brought into being at a stroke by the completion of this building, is so far just an administrative artifice: three characterless municipalities have been amalgamated, a central spot has been nominated, a competition held and now an ambitious building like a crash course in European, mostly Italian, urban culture, erected.

Fortunately the architects, Ed Jones and Michael Kirkland, are jokers as well as orators. Unlike most ventures of this kind, this town centre is no one's personal monument, but a crowding together of many civic ideas in the form of pediments, rostrums, alleys, amphitheatres, cylinders, cubes. The crowding is unnecessary but powerful in this

Pienza, in Tuscany, was renamed and given a new centre, with cathedral and papal palace (*left*), by Pope Pius II to commemorate his own birthplace. The new town of Richelieu (*right*), founded by the great cardinal, has outlasted the château that was its cause.

urban Mount Rushmore: unlike a true authoritarian dictum it doesn't aim to inhibit other monumental gestures but to spur them on.

Perhaps many projectors of ideal cities would be happy to see others take up the torch and carry the edges of the monumental precincts outward. The Pope who decided to turn his sleepy birthplace into a mini-Rome, renamed Pienza after himself, managed to spawn only a few private palaces, built near his own by other absentee cardinals, his cronies and protégés. Pienza today is still a rustic with a gleaming artificial heart, tissue it has rejected in the sense that it makes no effort to ease the transition with scaled down echoes in somnolent adjoining streets of the throbbing central pomposity.

Pienza is different too because the imported ideas are not even genuine in the central square. The cathedral is badly built and unfortunately placed, on the edge of a ravine into which it has been slipping ever since. The Piccolomini Pope's palace looks as if it was thrown up in a weekend – shortcuts are repeatedly evident: rustication is painted on in the internal court, and a series of arcades which don't match the side elevation are carelessly plastered across the back.

'Potemkin village' was a term coined from a Russian minister's way of greasing the empress's progress through Russia by building canvas mock-ups of thriving villages along the royal route, creating a false impression of the country's health. Pienza is a Potemkin village created with oneself as the object, a delusive urbanity in which it is hard to

imagine Pius spending many tranquil hours. Most embarrassing of all, it is only nine miles from Montepulciano where one can sample the truest Renaissance grandeur on the modest scale he was thinking of, palace after palace in a triumphal route more exquisite than anything in Rome.

The desire to found a city came over Cardinal Richelieu too, and the spot was chosen in somewhat the same way Pius picked Pienza, by personal association. The new town of Richelieu on the site of the old estate village abutted the park of his huge new château whose contents are now long ago dispersed and its buildings demolished. The town survives; though it has always been too big (its preservation), we notice only its smallness. The nearest model for this miniature city buried in the Poitou is Paris; it is a sample of urbanity more perfect than the real thing can ever be. From the triumphal gate at one end of the central spine one can look to the gate at the other, so Richelieu comes nearest to a complete city *at a glance*. It has one of everything – one church, one market, one back street on either side of the spine (and one alley just beyond that). Yet, reduced so to essentials, it didn't go far enough, for in this arbitrary spot, they needed no city at all. Now one savours its backwaterish disrepair, no motive to expand it, barely to maintain it, so it is held fast in time, reaching us intact because it failed.

Ledoux had a solider starting point for his ideal community in the forests of the Jura, a royal saltworks which had to be near a plentiful supply of firewood. So the sylvan metropolis, a geometrical garden

city, found an industrial excuse. In the end the saltworks and workers' housing were all that got built, but the architect went on projecting further rings of his solar system, further pages in his architectural encyclopedia long after the practical need had ceased.

The core is already symbolic and a depiction of infinitude. Work forms the centre of this diagram of human existence, but work so sublimed into metaphysics, we must marvel it functioned even as long as it did (the advent of canals soon made the remote location unnecessary). It begins with a formal announcement, a gatehouse behind a massive, unpedimented portico of the purest Doric.

One senses from afar that under this shelter something is awry. The columns shield a wild, rusticated front like a grotto, nature imprisoned in culture like a controlled industrial explosion. One traverses this ordeal and exits to a vastness, a great half-circle of empty space along whose edges all the town's buildings take up their places. It is the emptiness of sublime thoughts or sublime vacancy of mind.

Many of Ledoux's most stirring ideas have been emptied or half emptied of content in this way, like the hoopmaker's house consisting of two intersecting cylindrical sections raised on a hollow podium. He is forced to become his job, inhabiting the crossroads down which his hoops run, and contriving to fit his life into the solid left over around the edges of this depiction of void, a giant hoop held up to expose his life to continual fierce inspection.

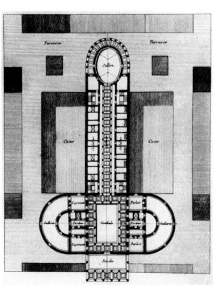

Ledoux's ideal city of Chaux is symbolic social engineering carried to its limit. *Left:* the complete scheme (only the first semi-circle was built). *Above:* the hoop-maker's house. *Right:* the 'house of sexual instruction'.

A dissimilar job is matched by a similar form. The river supervisor's house is another hoop, extended to make a section of pipe, through which his charge the river flows. So, like Kafka's prisoner, he is always learning the lesson of his life, can never turn away from it, and returning home comes even nearer to the constant din of his responsibility. In any other hands one would say it was an architecture of depiction not use: Ledoux is determined that the first should somehow ingest the second.

He projected a profane temple where the apotheosis of this theory would occur. Not for him idle rituals without practical result. In his Temple of Love the rite was copulation. But social and biological narratives were aligned in a bizarre way, and the history of the individual urge was matched to the journey of a sperm.

The building reveals itself nakedly only in plan; exterior elevations drew a modest veil over the tumultuous activities carried out within. The man pursued the woman at an accelerating pace from the bulging anterooms near the entrance, through the monumental shaft, to the private sanctuaries ranged round the head. Finally the sated pair exited at the top. It will be noted that one sex provides the model for both, and that the scenario says private desire is to the community as ejaculation is to the individual. The symbolism would be more satisfying to male participants; for them the two ranges of meaning might occasionally come together. The woman on the other hand might feel more a pawn than ever, subjected to this architectural stylization of male anatomy.

It may be retorted that this was a brothel not a connubial chamber, yet Ledoux's ideality does rather brothelize most experience so that it is publicized and becomes professional, whether it was really tending that way or not. When houses depict the inhabitants and the city plan plots the lives within, the population divides into mechanical caricatures and sullen prisoners.

Strangely enough, a few small American religious communities came nearest to realizing Ledoux-like rationality over an extended period. A rationality which usually had its limits – the Shakers were fiercely celibate, and so after a surprisingly long life (150 years) became extinct. Now we value them for the purity of their domestic implements and furnishings, which seem ultra-practical, a deification of function very appealing to modern hearts, but deeply celibate. The Shaker mind abhors impingement, crowding, touching. It is abnormally fastidious, so the problems of cleaning and putting things away assume untoward prominence. Shaker tidiness is permanent, not temporary. Here life is an unending prayer of everything in its place, not occasional flurries of devotion to order. So the rows of pegs at eye level on which objects of every description are hung become the main decorative system in rooms, like a classical frieze or a flower-border.

From the air, nineteenth-century mill-towns often look as if Shakers would be at home there. Identical houses form pleasingly uniform rows, everything in its place, and each street like another, as would be, ideally, the goods which the operatives turned out in their factories. For hundreds of years ideal cities had meant applications of rationality to the mess men had made of their communal lives. Then with the convulsion we call the Industrial Revolution it quickly became feasible to introduce unheard of uniformity in manufactured objects, including bricks, slates, moldings, and the other stuff of architecture. At the same time it became socially desirable, some thought, to impose a matching uniformity on the lives of workers.

This is a telescopic bridge over some very painful experience, meant to give a rudimentary sense of why ideal communities after a certain point in the last century are anti-rational and apparently regressive. The Arts and Crafts movement idealized the English village untouched by the machine age, and eventually we find Gimson, the Barnsleys and others actually moving to one, Sapperton in the Cotswolds, a region which remained somewhat isolated because of the hilly terrain, from which had come the building stone which assured that old structures decayed more slowly. There were deep reasons in the landscape, then, for settling here, but from our vantage the scheme, which included

The architecture and furniture of Shaker communities in America express an extreme form of restraint.

training country people in abandoned techniques, smacks of theatre, a play in period costume.

By comparison with some of their descendants it was authentic and unregulated. Another artists' commune at Darmstadt was more like an eighteenth-century landowner's planned village than a free community. Sponsored by the Grand Duke of Hesse, it had its esthetic dictator, Olbrich, to whom it looked perfectly organic. If such unities are proved by their dissidents, Darmstadt soon had those.

Dream villages did not remain the property of artists. The English garden suburb brought the ideal to a wider public. The social history of these places is undoubtedly the most interesting part, and still remains to be adequately treated, but perhaps how wide that public was will always be debated.

The founder of the greatest aesthetic success among garden suburbs, the one at Hampstead, imagined it as a place where all classes would mingle. Simple working-class flats were given a portion of the territory, and disguised to look a little less subdivided than they were. At this point

one fears the eighteenth-century estate village might be truer ancestor of the suburb than anyone will say. When one sees the little cloister of garages, with chauffeurs' quarters above each one, all veiled from the more decorous houses by a diagonal avenue of trees, one feels catapulted into positively feudal times.

The car has been the downfall of this if not other suburbs. Its projectors closed their eyes to it, and now interpolated garages have undone a great deal of their careful planning. For, like a ha-ha, Hampstead Garden Suburb is remarkable for what isn't there or at least for what you don't see. You don't see too many other houses from your own, you see no walls and fences, only low hedges (a country feature, though these are hedges not hedgerows) and occasional distant views. You don't often see adjacent houses the same, and you rarely see streets running uninterrupted for long, but various forms of enfolding and hiatus – closes, cul de sacs, staggered rows. Parker and Unwin, its main planners, had made careful studies of unplanned settlements and buildings, and from these obsolete barns and hamlets had extracted a system which could be applied by architects to produce intelligent artlessness like an updated form of the eighteenth-century landscape garden. To this day it gives us frequently the sense we are miles from London.

Hampstead Garden Suburb, near London (*left*), was intended to be an ideal mix of social classes living in harmony with each other and their surroundings. At Portmeirion, in North Wales (*right*), Clough Williams-Ellis created a personal fantasy, partly original, partly a reassembly of older buildings.

In spite of its communal preachments the movement was profoundly anti-urban, and as those who have lived in them know, its modern suburb-descendants have been the death of cities. By an even stranger irony, to the 1960s the suburb had come to stand for the most crushing uniformity of life, and communes sprang up in various isolated spots – northern California, Wales – a further stage in the suburb-ideal which hated suburbs even more than cities.

Its inventor's first idea for Portmeirion was that it needed to be built on an island, so he went looking for one and found the peninsula it is on, which he had long known and isn't many miles from his old family home, but more public in its placing. Clough Williams-Ellis describes this fictional town charmingly as what he had always wanted to do, following no dictates but his own. Yet it is a strangely historicist fantasy to stand for the last word in private wilfulness, like one of Liszt's pastiches from a well-known opera, reduced in scale and magnified in wayward expressiveness when brought down to the piano alone.

Portmeirion is an assemblage of definite flavours which make an imponderable whole. Clough Williams-Ellis doesn't hesitate to blend his differing provenances until even experts can't keep them straight, to put a seventeenth-century English ceiling, saved from a demolished house, in a German town hall, or to make the upper half of a rescued

Norman Shaw chimneypiece into the Plateresque porch for a Spanish church so small it is merely a lookout.

The whole 'village' is a little haven of impossibility – the designer's claim it was to wake people to the merits of architecture is window dressing like Disneyland's or Williamsburg's aspirations to give lessons in the American way. Portmeirion may be the quietest and most serious of the three, but it still teases the visitor by playing only snatches of tunes and letting him do the rest. Which is to say that anyone who hasn't been to Italy and Spain before he comes to Wales will find it rather thin, not realizing that these miniature piazzas and baby-steepnesses have their greater exemplars in climes where brightness is brought by the sun and not by pink and yellow paint. More than any continuously inhabited place (the most revealing moment in the whole day at Disneyland is closing time, when the artificially curving streets are methodically emptied of people) these play cities are derivative, imitations of something known first elsewhere. A Mediterranean town in Wales, Venice in Florida, the eighteenth century in modern Virginia, how near can one come to believing it, is the question the visitor keeps playing with until he decides he's had a surfeit of such fun.

By some twist of logic Williamsburg presents itself as more serious and realistic because it has its candlemakers and unpaved lanes, because inharmonious later growth has been demolished leaving gap-toothed spaces now filled with replicas of eighteenth-century gardens. Realer? It is a cut-away view of eighteenth-century life, exhibiting workings which churn away there in midair, unengaged or unbounded along the whole side from which we peer in. Visiting Williamsburg is like being an extra in a movie, fun but less historical than reading a good history. Blasphemy it sounds in American ears, but there are some things you can't do yourself; driving down Colonial Parkway into the eighteenth century is one.

Williamsburg is a child of the 1930s, and the parkways which link it with even more imaginary sites at Jamestown and Yorktown are among the most successful idealizations of that era, which make travel without markers or visible destination the most beautiful experience. The original Disneyland, opened in 1955, and now a period piece, also makes getting there an important part of the fun.

But in this case one finds one's way through the sprawl of suburban LA, the first sprawl in the world which wasn't justified by a rich central core, which was that democratic milestone, autonomous sprawl. One arrives at the entrance to Disneyland . . . and boards the monorail which takes one on a wordy circuit of vast parking lots, cleverly circles the

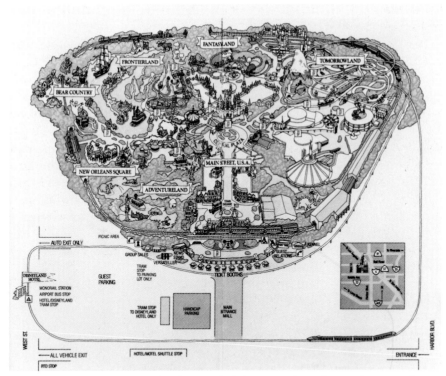

Disneyland, near Los Angeles, the ultimate ideal city, a marriage of entertainment and profit.

terrain tasting each of the 'Lands' within the Land, like one who on returning home quickly runs through every room to make sure it is all in place. For the novice the shrewdness of this is not at once apparent. Since he doesn't know the extent of the territory he doesn't realize he has just seen it all.

Good maps of Disneyland are not, for good reason, provided. Like an eighteenth-century garden it expends its best energies concealing its bounds. Coming in, one has had the nearest thing to a map. One will keep referring to that glimpse of how it fits together in deciding where to turn next, but one can't recall it to examine what comes to matter most, the nature of the edges.

Disneyland, like the most intricate garden, fits so much into its small bounds you wonder where all these pirate caves can be. Underground is the answer and the secret of the fantastic density, so when emerging from one of the 'rides' in semi-darkness one feels most the place's power to represent human imagination with its overlapping powers which take no space, as Disneyland, so artfully threaded through itself, seems a physical impossibility.

It is a compelling prototype for many features of American life because it shows the whole world turned over to fiction and play. Half the restaurants and many of the shops in America are its descendants, part of a galloping 'recreationizing' of formerly straightforward activities. It is a breed of fun on which vast amounts have been spent: one could stage several operas with the glittering props of 'Pirates of the Caribbean' scattered through their deep tunnels like treasure lost in a mine. These visionary expenditures are not, as Walt Disney, calling to us from beyond the grave keeps insisting, his benefactions to his beloved America. For the money flowed out only to return in greater floods. Now very little money changes hands within the sacred circle of enjoyment, but Disney's greatest gift to the country remains the discovery that fun pays so handsomely. In Disneyland Pleasure and Commerce walk happily hand in hand.

One may leave Laon, in northern France, wondering how one will recompense the world for providing one with such amusement. It is one of the perfect cities of tourism, an anti-rational ideal like Disneyland, crystallized, like all the most exquisite urban relics, on a hilltop, with its cathedral a more fabulous gem perched *on it*, a muscular crystal which contains more than one can ever properly inhabit or even list. At Disneyland one comes out owing no one anything, though one has probably not had as much fun as one should. At Laon one contracts a debt, which one might discharge by writing a novel about the relation between the high old town and the sprawling new one at its base, unravelling the dependence of the art one came hoping to skim from the top on the commerce one wanted to leave ignored lower down. And the difference between the two, Laon and Disneyland, may come down to the choice between fooling oneself or being fooled.

CHAPTER IV

Ruins

RUINS ARE IDEAL: the perceiver's attitudes count so heavily that one is tempted to say ruins are a way of seeing. Of course they actually exist, but since the eighteenth century they are never just problems of maintenance. Rather, practically any human thing slipping into dereliction, the forecast of ruin, engages our feelings about where we see ourselves in history, early or late, and (in poignant cases) our feelings about how the world will end.

The ruin mentality appears frivolous, fixated on surface not substance. It is in fact deeply pessimistic, counting more ancestors than descendants, sure without thinking that it inhabits a decadent phase. Feelings about decadence are some of the most twisted and interesting in all culture, and by our taste for ruins we affirm our belief in decadence, our half-voluntary imprisonment in it. Ruins are models or heralds of the disintegrating mind and collapsing principles of the age after the end of stable belief, the half-loved companions of post-religious man haunted by ghosts of faith.

In England the ruin taste starts in country churchyards not classical digs, and Bentley's illustrations to Gray's poem are a codification of this picturesque enthusiasm. One discovers a healthy mistrust of the metropolis, or a morbid prowling among tombs, obsessed with crannies and backwaters. The aesthetic preferences match these social refusals or perversions: favouring incompletion or asymmetry, focusing on silhouette or a shaggy edge not solidity or mass. The ruin taste is an eccentric branch or twig of rococo, which in England threatened to run away with the plant. There it remained a style with a powerful literary bias, always coming loaded with narrative.

In Rome a process took place which looks diametrically different from the English churchifying of the garden, the house, and last, but most profound of all, the English Protestant church itself. There in Rome, the capital of ruin, monks' cells were turned into imaginary secular, or even worse, pagan ruins. Clérisseau made his famous ruin-

room in the convent at Trinità dei Monti for two French priests, an idea so startling and so attuned to some longing of the age that it was often copied.

Building ruins in Rome might seem a waste of effort, but the point was that one could comfortably inhabit this one, getting all the beauty of disorder without the inconvenience. A whole wall of the room had given way and let in the sky, and the roof was no more than a few crooked planks between which huge chinks seemed to admit the sun. The other walls were patched together of sarcophagi, windows pierced through at later date, and mouldering stone whose deficiencies were plugged with moss and tufts of fern.

One realized immediately of course that all the instability was only painted on, and that under the scenic effect subsisted dependable walls. One didn't hesitate either to seat oneself on the rough upended-capital chairs, drawing them up to the damaged cornice = table or the shattered sarcophagus = desk, and one played with the monks' dog after coaxing him from his kennel, a toppled urn. This isn't a Crusoe-dream of ingenious use, happy to find that exotic plants provide brooms or buckets through eccentricities of form, but an opposing dream of total camouflage of function, where everything is accident in a will-less aftermath.

Piranesi was the greatest propagandist of this view of our historical situation. He delights to see historical wealth as a rubbish heap of useless, and more importantly, indecipherable bits. Gemlike remnants of a great age – busts, reliefs, urns – are smothered in or seen generating floods of foliage or spring-water. Stone, in the course of decay, comes to look like

something else, softer, more organic, as if the world was or will be a creature.

Irrational modes of organization are gaining ground: main axes are forgotten, the most preposterous disproportions given their head, and one gets lost in a phantasmagoric density where the effort to keep one's bearings is doomed. For Piranesi, prisons are a release into freer spatial experiment, but all spaces are in some sense prisons, entered voluntarily in high anticipation of their pleasing confusions.

He is one of the most persuasive paper-architects, and from him many have learned that they prefer shams to the truth, that the most prized forms of mental freedom require a certain insulation from reality. One becomes one's own prisoner. Mock-ruins are thus not always a substitute or second-best for the real ones one can't command, though for simpler minds they may be. This is a ticklish question, however, since most ruins have been helped along, arrested, added to, or subtracted from. There are shams with authentic bits dotted among the fresher stones to lend them authority, or actual abbeys whose most entertaining or usable spaces are later improvements.

But essentially it is fair to say that sham ruins were often a purposeful misuse of religion, not a simple attempt to mislead. One built the shadow of a church – a tower and part of a wall say – with a pompous doorway which led nowhere but the other side of the wall, and one had from the beginning nothing but mock terror and mock solemnity, the shell or carapace of belief, a rococo *version* of feelings of which the main body had long ago vanished, as if eaten away from inside by some process of organic decay.

At other times medieval forms are filled with new (and inappropriate) functions: at Woodbridge Lodge, Rendlesham, in Suffolk an oversized Gothic finial lies directly on the ground like a trivial remnant from an enormous cathedral, the rest of which is nowhere to be seen. In an actual Gothic building it would have formed the uninhabited terminal of a large aspiring element, silhouetted against the sky and causing us to crane up at it. Now homely doors and windows poked in its sides show it is a gatekeeper's house, and when we notice smoke issuing from the point where all its flying buttresses meet, we realize that these contain the chimney flues.

This lodge is only an awkward instance of a widespread fad, the cult of the fragment, which is a way of turning the painful accident of ruin to positive esthetic point. Landscapes like the Woodbridge Lodge is set in are often dotted with half hidden treasures, a dispersed museum of Gothic relics stumbled upon with little shocks of discovery.

Woodbridge Lodge,
Rendlesham, in Suffolk,
the gamekeeper's house
disguised as the crown of
a Gothic church tower. It
was built about 1820.

One of the best mature fruits of the ruin craze occurs unexpectedly in a London terrace house, which the architect John Soane cobbled together over many years for himself, far from a single conception, more like a monstrous growth, which continues to develop until the very day its inhabitant dies.

The plan shows that what seems on the outside, and is at the front, a single unit in width, spreads in the back to three – an unclassical, irregular progress. What were only hints in preliminary rooms become consuming obsessions in the row of study-rooms or museums which engulf the rear of the house. These are in any ordinary physical sense functionless spaces, for they are too full of Soane's various collections to permit any but mental activity.

At the heart of it is the Dome, a continuous space cut through three floors, made of discontinuities, of which the model is ruin not building, and where the figmental underlying structure is drastically obscured by corruscating fragments of many sizes and sorts, chunks of huge cornice, roof ornaments, colossal heads or feet, urns, and chaotic syllables of vegetable scroll-work.

All these objects (ancient marble, modern plaster, Gothic wood tumbled randomly together) float as if in some phantasmagoric dream, as if all the ghosts from nearby graves (the lower reaches of this house

103

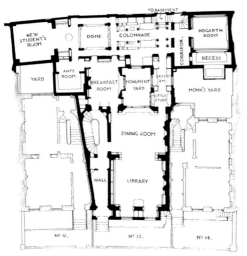

Sir John Soane's house in Lincoln's Inn Fields, London. *Right:* the Dome. *Above:* plan of the house and its courtyard.

contain Egyptian, monkish, and classical tombs) have been summoned at once and come together in strange conglomerate life. Soane conjures up an animated vision of the past that treads very near to madness, in which categories fail and hierarchies collapse.

This architect knew what he was doing of course; it was a calculated transport, a picturesque effect which conflated mausoleum and museum, individual and cultural memorial, to make a lavish monument or house for Memory. Which is also the lesson of his more purely architectural conceptions, where the lightly traced classical forms, like inscriptions which fade when the viewer comes near (an effect archaeologists in the field have commented on), signifies a tenuous hold on one's historical models or ancestral memories.

At their purest, in the Breakfast room next to the Dome, Soane's spaces are spectral, whose walls dissolve in light, ceilings float, and rooms come apart into bits of mirror, picture, and coloured glass making the eye dart restlessly, feasting, wandering, like the unattached foreign tourist in Rome. It is the most subtle and complete domestication of those ephemeral sensations of the serious traveller into plastic permanence.

To this day these spaces are enigmatic and hard to grasp, for reasons allied to what we feel before perfunctory modern ruin-follies which seem commercially motivated. Who would have thought that contemporary American shoppers could entertain simultaneously the consumer's fiction of perpetual shiny function and fantasies of decay? But that must be what happens at the various bizarre designs by SITE for the shopping mall stores of Best Products. The whole series adds up like Piranesi's connected studies of nearly indistinguishable Roman ruins. In the Best stores the disease of ruin has attacked only a small portion of the fabric, invariably near the entrance, leaving the rest unaffected so far and no different from standard mall blandness. Debates could be held over whether the remainder seems threatened, or the eccentricity no herald but a unique carbuncle which, it is true, taunts the spectator with hints that collapse is about to include him, for the wall overhead cascades downward, leaving a V subtracted from the flat stretch of masonry, its slipped mass coming toward us like the scree of a disintegrating cliff.

The great joke here is the enforced stillness. The fall of the mighty is caught in its headlong course like the violence in a movie still, so that we feel relatively sure we can go on watching the mass *about* to come to rest on the ground like the satyr on the urn about to catch the maiden he

Best Products Stores, Houston, Texas: a modern commercial building that uses the ruin as a sophisticated game.

pursues. And so the consumer is subliminally assured that death can be held at bay while he makes another purchase. Why not play the game, it says to him, since that is all it is? An entirely secular view of last realities suits the tourist whose foreign lands are merchandise.

It isn't usual to classify ruins, like deaths, according to how they occur, as convulsive or gradual, though perhaps if one's dead remained above ground one would come to a different view of that too. Very seldom do we know how a building fell into ruin, and assume it is a single repeated process. One may be surprised to observe that the ragged edge left on a large apartment block by a gas explosion is picturesque, or to enjoy a visit to a village unpeopled by an earthquake. In these the emptiness came all at once, which usually accumulates over years. Occasionally one gets glimpses of a ruination made up of an infinitude of tiny gradations, like a human decline, which if nothing puts a stop to it, reminds one of a range of hills, a fresh horror appearing every morning to replace the previous sign of the loved being's long slide into decrepitude and incapacity.

We need a careful series of the degrees of ruin like a paint chart or colour wheel as one adds further minute amounts of white (that is, of passage) to the basic tone. The common opinion is that the most sublime ones don't speak very clearly of mundane uses. *There* functions will rarely be recognized by an unexpert eye. One can tell only that this is something formerly articulated, now sinking back into the landscape. One can tell because odd bits of refinement jump out at one, the fluting of a ragged section of column, say, which experience gathered elsewhere helps one know the use of. At a place like Delos one has mostly a jabber of fragments, discontinuity for which there is no deliberate literary parallel before Dada collages, and it is doubtful even then if Heartfield's hubbubs of typography are really to be seen as pure line, and not rather as having something to do with language, which has died or lost its meaning, but remains language still, reminding one of the days in which it appeared in working order.

This is one extreme of ruin, familiar from some of the most prestigious classical sites like Leptis Magna in Libya, of a body so finely pulverized it seems pure *bit*, like a smashed pot or torn paper no one will think it worthwhile to piece back together. That is the commonsensical opinion, at least, but it is never safe to decide at what level of minuteness human attention will cry enough. Increasing crowds of scholars, numerous as the sands these ruins are being reduced to, make possible, even obligatory, intense cultivation of relic-rich soil which earlier centuries couldn't spare the time for.

Whereas the rubbish of the past has meaningful associations for us, today's rubbish seems simply a nuisance. Portobello Road, London, at the end of a busy Saturday.

Ordinary litter, such as accumulates in certain spots which are neither city nor country, or in streets where the garbagemen are on strike, is formally similar, but does not cause the same pleasure as the more hygenic rubbish of classical sites. Is it only prejudice which prevents such appreciation? Are we not watching the same degeneration at a different speed? But as has often been remarked the sense of smell is not a welcome participant in most art-experience. It cannot be a high spiritual moment if detectable odours are present, is what most people think; incense has seemed a questionable accompaniment of religious cere-mony, at least in the West. The Indian predilection for it is like a whiff of corruption and sign of confusions between high and low spiritual states, moving towards feature-less oneness.

Perhaps if one chose something of more austere formal composition, sorted not random rubbish, one could approach Greek grandeur? Searching for a more dignified effect among the consistency of a TV graveyard, say, one will succeed only if one has forgotten what TV's are, and sees the nobility in this cascade of dissolution. It is essentially our ignorance and not our knowledge which stirs us before the Greek fragments. Like the most moving Greek sculpture, now less than a shadow of its old self, the best classical sites are architecture without architects, where roles have been reversed, and landscape has reasserted itself over buildings. They are important not for helping us reconstruct past civilization but for assuring us there will always be something bigger than that. Without really leaving it behind, they show us that the human culture which constrains and fascinates us is not all there is in the world, and that one can transcend the human, simply by following art over the edge into dissolution.

Fuseli's *Artist Moved by the Grandeur of Ancient Ruins* shows a figure in a state of utter dejection dwarfed and enclosed by selected bits of a colossus, which though larger and hence more powerful than he, is in its dismemberment equally ineffectual. The past is conceived as a figure or being, now reduced to abstraction and monstrosity. The artist is part and not part of the collapse: his posture echoes the cascading form familiar in many scenes of ruin, but for all his solidarity with the fallen giant he remains apart, neither buried nor assimilated, revelling now in a fit of melancholy which will pass.

This picture is a clear portrayal of ruin as a psychic state. The artist is smaller but his feelings dominate the scene. Even Rome is dwarfed by the intensity of our projections onto it, and everyone secretly feels when confronted by obliteration of the above-ground traces of his memories that it is mainly a *personal* loss. When a childhood scene is cleared to make way for something else or perhaps for nothing else, one's first thought is not of those who lived there last, one's successors, but of one's old sensations which are now a book abruptly closed. In Fuseli's picture the little node of consciousness validates the whole, creating a subject where otherwise there would be none.

When we return to the summer camp, now bulldozed and reverting to forest, of which we remember principally the strange foreign murals on the lecture hall walls, we feel betrayed. At some point in the past, we don't know when, this memory which has its fixed place in our museum, was undermined and left dangling in air like a bit of architectural ornament under which the supporting timbers have rotted, leaving it no option but to fall. Our memory has been senselessly delayed in feeling the shock.

If even the vividest memories are a sort of ruin, in which parts but not all of some functional construction are preserved, according to a logic as inscrutable as the action of weather on buildings, the rememberer often has a reassuring sense that he could reconstruct the original artefact more fully, simply by returning to the scene of it. But the more distant and previous the scene, the more likely to have undergone change.

In Fuseli's *Artist Moved by the Grandeur of Ancient Ruins*, the fragments of a colossal statue (in fact of Constantine and now in the Capitoline Museum) are crushing in their scale and authority.

Maybe the name for such alterations is the clean opposite of ruin. How can one sit down and mope, contemplating the grandeur of one's vanished past, beside or propped against what isn't there? One of the most reliable features of my childhood was a wall which became scalable only as I got bigger, which blocked the end of the street and ran as far as you could see in either direction. Behind it was a realm more interesting than anything outside, an abandoned estate where one could hallucinate overgrown statues, or greenhouses run wild, connected by brick passages under a drive to caverns full of flowerpots. As one got bolder one could follow half obliterated paths to the house which lay at the centre of the labyrinth, which one succeeded in arriving at one time in three.

But the best part took place outside the wall. During the week, we passed it planning our weekend assaults. When outside you grew uncertain what it was like within, though by then we had climbed it many times. Now Thornwald (its name, from the twisted local thorn trees which had colonized our lawn too) is a public park, and the house an old people's home. Ten years ago the wall came down, inconsistent with new openness and availability, and dangerous and liable to result in lawsuits against the town (not something the absent owner had given a thought to).

Now from our house (no longer ours) you see right in: trees whose tops showed over the wall are exposed along their whole height; the cleared oval before the woods begin, formerly a forbidden room, the place one was most likely to be caught by the caretaker, has no shape and gapes witlessly at you along a whole stretch of road. Now one can drive down the drive, through gates which were always locked, and doesn't need to dodge in and out of the fringing forest. Now I know exactly how various features along this ride are related to each other, that were formerly monsters in a nightmare or funhouse which could loom up when least expected in an order I was never sure of, because I never felt safe enough just to walk down this path, but had to invent a complex route which had as its aim my concealment, as its result my befuddlement.

The town is proud to have rescued the Sadler estate from ruin, and it is true that now you sometimes pass people walking there, though it is really too far from town to be the right place for a park. Rehabilitated, it has *become* a ruin, of a dispiriting sort, losing its history and its defining edge. But it would be hard to explain for much longer, the unattentive owner now dead, what this vast closed space was being saved for.

It was a private theatre or psychomachia in which a generation of children imagined the contest between nature and a vanished mankind, as if though young they had been able to enter the world after the real makers and creators had passed, to see therefore the work losing its character, so that potting sheds could be mistaken for the headquarters of cults, and wine-cellars for burial vaults. All the historical possibilities they'd ever heard of seemed likely inhabitants of the puny structures which dotted this woodland, where one could never be sure that the best features weren't pure accident. It was one of the oldest dreams come true, a world created or left behind for them alone, not yet or no longer inhabited by the tiresome grownups who had been required to build it.

There was a phrase current in 1950s and 60s America, urban *renewal*, which meant flattening the old parts of cities. When this was done on the widest scale, as in St Louis, it left a strange zone of high grass and expressways between the commercial district and the first streets of houses. In St Louis it was easy to gauge how much had been removed in this way, because in the series of numbered streets about fifteen were simply missing. Perhaps before long will come the time for archaeological reconstruction of the vanished parts. By then the abdication which made destruction possible will seem almost incomprehensible, like missing decades in a history.

At any given moment there are historical blind spots, which is to say bits of the past which have no character we can detect and therefore look like nothing at all. The 1950s are just emerging from this kind of non-existence, and doubtless in the last ten years many big 1950s artefacts have disappeared without anyone's really noticing their departure. There are still a few remnants of the Festival of Britain lurking not very conspicuously in Battersea Park, probably safer for not looking like much of anything, a series of shallow pools dotted with flagpoles and framed by viewing pavilions like bus shelters.

Animated spaces exist nearby, while this is deserted, which makes it look as if it is happening a long time ago, like Pompeii. One has to think hard to recall how short a time has passed since it was the last word in newness, so crumbly are all the concrete edges, so mottled the light blue paint which smacked of fresh sea breezes. Here the poignancy is that modernity has so soon fallen into irrelevance and will only survive through the negligence of those who live in a different age. One thinks the Battersea relics are mainly amusing, and doesn't work out that it is one's own childhood which is now infinitely remote, a historical fact on the verge of extinction.

The paintings of Caspar David Friedrich express more powerfully than any others the loneliness of those from whom their history recedes at breakneck pace, because when he worked it was a fresh fact. His emptinesses are loaded because not comfortably accepted, but newly felt. Perhaps they have lain there unremarked until he comes and says 'it is over' – the world is no longer inhabited, its informing spirit fled.

When Friedrich paints a ruin, it is what remains after a spiritual bomb has exploded, leaving both man and nature shattered. Grave markers and figures are confused, every edge harsh as if the world's discourse were broken off in mid sentence. It is a strongly negative view of ruin, very clear headed, as if one measured the proportion of building still standing, and made out a receipt for the rest.

In the very first moments after the life has fled, the ones he paints, one is still conscious that these trees, mounds, huts, recently had souls and now do not. It is a landscape strewn with superstitions, in uninsistent forms which it takes a sharp eyed visitor to pick out. Friedrich's special quality is to reverence superstitions without believing them, to relish the fact of them without letting them capture him. So like ruin-lovers he is an early anthropologist, student not worshipper, viewing it all from a great remove.

He comes at the beginning of a process by no means complete. To feel that culture lies in ruins can sometimes be a way of saying its motive force or conviction wanes or is lost. Friedrich's disillusionment, more sweeping, sees this process spreading to the natural world. Having come to feel religion an artifice and civilization a kind of self deception, nineteenth-century man had only a short distance to travel in order to think that physical reality too was another mechanism, in which it was childish to speak of 'being at home'. Home was an invented idea which didn't really belong anywhere and was utterly dependent on where one decided to put it.

Geologists continued to regard the world as a ruin after they had stopped thinking it had formerly meant anything uplifting, or ever been a more coherent building than now. This was simply the wishful metaphor, like a child's toy, which grown men found it hard to lay aside entirely. Friedrich is an early presenter of religion as a set of natural metaphors; to him all man's hopes are buried in landscape. He paints scenes of devastation which seem harmonious rooms to many and alarming voids to a few, which is simply to say that metaphysical longings are rarer now than they once were.

Friedrich's trees have been pollarded by old age or tempest. It is a natural kind of distress, yet like deliberate pruning it makes one hallucinate the missing bits. So just-pollarded trees can sometimes produce an unlooked for picturesque effect: they are incompletely drawn toward an architectural idea. When on the other hand an architect builds something like pollarded trees, the effect is unruly and natural. Gaudi's canted columns fading into the rugged roof at Parc Guell introduce us to the problem from the other side; we could almost forget they were made by an architect. Without him a slope, with him a complicated stepped affair, one offshoot of which is an obscure refuge under this row of tree-columns growing into a roof, which bends to make a wall, which when it reaches the ground near the columns, throws up a lip we use as a bench to look out through the columns at the greenery.

Gaudi has made a continuity of all the basic elements of architecture, which thus feel abnormally at home in the world. Architecture reabsorbed by nature or trees maturing into columns – intention loses itself in instinct, the world undivided once more, in which the state of ruin feels temporarily impossible, for in nature all which is no longer capable of growth supports growth, and besides, we haven't come to the moment of failing vitality in this particular structure. Though it is nothing but different kinds of masonry, it resembles successively rugged

Caspar David Friedrich's *Abbey in an Oak Forest*. The church, the trees, humanity itself, are in ruins.

bark, a blanket of leaves, and cracked clay like an old and water-starved skin. Which is to say that the very artifice is metamorphic and a sign of vitality, so conceived that it seems life not death.

But it resembles petrified forms like tree stumps turned to coal, which are relics in a later material of an earlier form, exhibiting the broken edges and infinite textural differences which distinguish ruins from kept-up structures, which often distinguish age from youth or sickness from health. So *aged* olive trees are more interesting than young, to seekers after picturesque sensations, so mountains in obvious states of decay than ones shrouded in trees.

Among some of the most favoured mountains in Britain the sensation can suddenly overcome one of a world in ruins, of absolute torrents of rubble like wide roads of it. Their irregularity, complex and fascinating as it is, does not explain why the mountains' shape is so gripping, or why they keep us strongly occupied in some form of decipherment. Is it perhaps that we are reconstructing them, replacing, mentally, all the fallen pieces, trying to undo or re-experience the history of how they got that way? Yet this is a forlorn vision, and mountains are surely not loved for making us gloomy.

Mountains are the largest physical assertions on earth, so that scaling them one allies oneself with heroism. They are heroes and we are their echoes, or students who will learn their ways As we climb them we get further from anything we know, until by the force of their huge identities they blot out ours, a good avenue for subduing the self.

A favourite way of coping with the strangeness and size of mountains is to give parts of them human names as if they are ruined bits of a larger world, traces of a hero's life, like Devil's Punchbowl or Ossian's Cave. The second, at Glencoe, is a far-off Monet-impression of a cave, a blurred vaginal opening with no floor, on a Wagnerian scale. To make such a strong effect from the valley below it must be at least a hundred feet high. Or we may imagine that the old world-floor has been raised out of our reach, producing new inferior realms which we inhabit.

At the other end of the geological chain are silted plains or marshes like the ones at Cliffe in Kent which are the nearest thing to a literal model for the scenes at the end of *Great Expectations*. This is the kind of ruined landscape the convict emerged from and is now re-buried in, a Protean place where, as one life (or terrain) is broken down into

Geological ruin in Scottish mountains. *Far left:* Stac Polly, in Sutherland. *Left:* Ossian's Cave, Glencoe.

unrecognizability, another is born from the slime, fertilized by death. Lower reaches of large rivers are gloomy places because all the elements seem to be running out of energy. The earth becomes flatter, the river slower, the sky emptier. The fact that buildings and people are sparser, which has a simple explanation, we interpret as if it illustrated the operation of a curse. Like the mountaintop the marsh's edge seems land on the way to something else. Up to a point (the point where one needs to switch from boots to a boat) one applauds the disintegration of the landscape, one's normal perspective inverted: as in a crumbling wall, unsoundness makes all the incident.

Some amazing textures are achieved by the re-employment of old bits in later structures, like the re-use of pulverized bits of higher ground to create new landscapes lower down. San Salvatore at Spoleto resembles the aftermath of an architectural avalanche in a few striking details. As often happened in Italy Roman remains have been looted to supply rich trimmings for a rude Christian structure. Fluted columns are a favoured subject for such treatment, and here columns borrowed from different antique buildings don't quite match.

Sometimes this is disguised by alternating smooth and ridged, or fat and thin ones, as if a rhythm not a consistency had been meant from the start. But at San Salvatore the desire to resurrect old ruins violates greater decorums still: bits of riotous vegetable cornice appear and disappear above eye level, collaged with other pieces of different scale, ending too soon because not enough remnants were found, clashing against a battered capital beneath or another section of cornice so rich it has been pressed into use as a capital.

All the columns reach to the same height, but as they are of different lengths this means that some fall short of meeting the ground beneath, gaps made up in different ways – with fatter bases, with sections of not-congruent columns, or strangest of all, with great lumps of cornice retaining their huge chipped teeth.

The walls beyond the arcade show there was no local dearth of building stone. So it would have been easier to fill the hiatuses in the collection of architectural rarities with inconspicuous modern replacement. That this wasn't done may show a consistency so fanatical that its results look inconsistent now, like the efforts of a searcher for a lost article who begins to forget more important things remembering that.

Modern visitors will see it with Piranesian eyes, but the mind at work here is almost the contrary of that dilettante mode. Richness in San Salvatore is not a contrived disorder, but true salvage, the earnest display of one's best. To their compiler, the fact that these remnants make a threadbare effect, of Crusoe-like inadequacy, is cause for chagrin not rejoicing.

The mystery may be cleared up at Bevagna where we come upon the doorframe of a Romanesque church made from a classical cornice turned ninety degrees, until the overhanging mass is converted into a vertical fringe which spreads from the door in widening ripples, like Romanesque portals made from scratch. Perhaps this perversion of purpose pleased its inventor, but more likely not – rather he would have felt humbled that his departed ancestors carved better when doing distant borders, than he could hope to match even on the greatest highlight of the building.

Piranesi collecting fragments rejoices in wealth; the Romanesque carver who adds small birds and terminal fillups to round off the borrowed stretch of pattern admits a lack: the time for excellence is past, our world is fallen like those buildings.

It is true that there are instances of older carved fragments immobilized in later walls like flies in amber, randomly, as if they have wandered in and got immured. Or collected together absentmindedly,

Vestiges of the past incorporated into a later building in Italy – San Salvatore, Spoleto.

as if someday someone might want these, so why not hang onto them? Or perhaps it is laziness which avoids cutting new stone.

Laziness is not what produced one of the bizarrest reliquaries of this kind, though who can be sure what it was instead? In the main street at Montepulciano, which is almost a museum of rustication, one comes to the Palazzo Bucelli, which is rusticated to shoulder height with a collection of Etruscan funerary urns packed in courses like giant bricks. Plainly it is only facing – front ends have been sheered from those convenient boxes and stacked to make this little mock cemetery. Might this be reverent not irreverent, an eccentric acknowledgment we build *on*, even *of* the bones of past civilizations, instead of heartless plundering which makes trinkets of other lives? Rustication, a prior or ruder cultural phase, is here grimly actualized as an earlier human generation.

For the most part the lids of the tombs are missing, which would often have carried a little model of the deceased lying down, leaning on one elbow. Such figures are always painfully compressed, the head too big for the body, torso too big for the legs, as if in a lingering wish to present him life-size when there isn't enough room to do so, as if the Etruscan imagination never caught up with the change the Romans brought from burial to cremation. The funeral wall at Montepulciano is a further reductio, ashes and covers of the urns discarded, and the saved faces fused together in a mercilessly crowded mosaic.

Such concentration, creating from forlorn ruin a kind of theatre audience now spectator at the affairs of a living street, though undeniably lively, is a profoundly unnatural historical effect. To some it seems a typically Italian confusion, turning private meditation to theatrical display, but one theory holds that the first theatre was a street, not in the sense that early itinerant shows were staged there, or Roman backdrops based on street façades, but that it is one of the mainsprings of drama in social life. The amphitheatre at Arles filled up with houses because people needed somewhere to live, not because they followed a theory of continuous spectacle or wanted to display themselves. Nevertheless one would have felt some of the old theatre feeling penetrating these precincts. It was still an arena, however defaced, and a primitive (though negative, being *filled*) version of the urban square.

At Lucca the amphitheatre had at one time grown more enmeshed in the urban fabric than it is now. In the nineteenth century (a plaque in its walls tells when and at whose instigation) most of the dwellings built into the thickness of the walls were left in place, but the curve of the amphitheatre was freed wherever possible, and everything clogging the central space removed.

The result is that modern inhabitants fill the position of the ancient audience and tourists straggling across the vacant ellipse provide a meagre spectacle, along with the scattered cars of the residents. It is

The Palazzo Bucelli, Montepulciano, which has fragments of Etruscan and Roman sculpture embedded in the wall.

The Piazza del Anfiteatro in Lucca preserves the shape of the old Roman amphitheatre on which its houses stand.

another of those effects of living in a world which used to be more thickly populated. The amphitheatre is still, as it always was, near the edge of Lucca, so the great square forms an unneeded exhibit, like a living Roman museum keeping up the pretence of being an active part of a real city.

Of all ruins Pompeii gives the strongest sense of absence, full of ghosts of its inhabitants, partly because so much is there, and complete streets of Roman buildings lead off into the distance. Of course the roofs are missing, crushed under the weight of ash. If it had been discovered in another place at another time this feature might have been replaced: one is still liable to forget that Pompeii got lost and needed to be rediscovered. So the most natural because most complete of ruins is like a corpse displayed above ground, and only possible through a lucky disaster.

That catastrophe has had the effect of making centuries of history shrink to nothing. We can have Pompeii because it didn't experience the

A street in Pompeii, a city not so much decayed as smothered and later brought back to life.

intervening years, a relic without a history. It is special for us insofar as it is not a ruin, but almost our contemporary, through an unhistorical trick of nature.

The most extensive of all ruins never actually fell into ruin, after the roofs fell like a protective blanket keeping even the most trivial objects and a certain number of the inhabitants in place until our arrival. So Pompeii never erupted, as many ruins have, pushing up through later constructions like an educational earthquake, the best example being the amphitheatre at Lecce which in working its way out to the surface laid waste the main square, an extreme case of ruins as the causes of ruin and even of complete destruction for those at the centre of the blast. One can thus lie under the weight of ruin as under a sterilizing curse, the earth having coughed up an undigested meal which piety insists we leave forever in place, as if the particular configurations left by the bombing of London had been considered sacred, and we went on forever thoughtfully skirting incomplete walls and blocked paths.

Coda: Industrial Ruins

To find Piranesi-sensations in the real world, which is to say ruins which are really our contemporaries, or at least near to us in time, we need to go to abandoned industrial buildings. If Piranesi were alive today, one of his favourite outings would be riding Amtrak from New York to Philadelphia, and he would always try to sit on the lefthand side of the train. After the marshes announcing New Jersey, threaded by monstrous impositions like the Pulaski Skyway, an earthbound elevated highway made of filthy metal, after this landscape-ruin full of herons and trash of mysterious origin, an alarming series begins, of disused factories empty except for watchmen whose cars appear from time to time, the only bright or fresh notes in a courtyard formerly full of activity, now evident only in remnants left behind and half rifled, or dumped later and giving false clues, or delivered in error and forgotten.

They are the most communicative sort of building, even when functioning and not, like the incontinent aged, letting things show on their clothes which should be kept inside the body. But even when working properly, industrial buildings are a little like that. Their produce or raw material is stacked alongside waiting for the next stage in the process.

It is obtuse to approach them as architecture pure and simple, when their real contribution is to be such unashamed anti-architecture, who add on new bits without thought of how they match the old, as if the designer had been given the measurements and no more, and had never visited the site before, during, or after construction.

Who would think unintentionality could have such interesting fruits? Unlike work of real architects, these buildings get better with everything which goes wrong, and every inappropriate alteration. They are places where cost constraints cause entertaining botches, where devices cobbled together in a hurry are more expressive than better ways of doing the job.

Ancient ruins vividly depict the passage of time, but it is now almost frozen. By noticing them we remove them from the buffeting stream. Industrial ruins are most special in this: though large and powerful they feel extremely vulnerable. No one is going to keep them just for a spectacle, so the richer they become as ruins, the nearer and surer their demolition approaches. Old ruins only *look* doomed anymore, these plants and factories *are*. They change from month to month; the peeling paint on the label where the company's name used to be, which one mistakes at first for a tangle of Chinese dragons in clouds, is a truly chance effect, not much slower to fall to pieces than the clouds it resembles. Industrial ruins are anonymous and we don't direct people to particular ones (like the endlessly long factory in Macclesfield Road, London EC1, with the Chinese scroll-label) because it would be the strangest freak if they lasted till those visitors came.

We savour them for whole ranges of breakage which would not be tolerated in an operating or presentable structure, because such events are real too, seem in fact realer than everything else because unwilled, pushing puny man aside. Broken and blocked windows, air extractors with sections missing, leaking water tanks stranded on roofs, are all harbingers of purposeful demolition. This ugliness does not become beautiful until one realizes that all these signs tell us it will be swept away.

One catches oneself admiring a grim old plant one would, not long ago, have hurried past, which is now a toothless killer some of whose limbs have been struck off, leaving dangling girders, bits of wall framing nothing, and the old tile floor now full of parked cars. Perhaps one's residual incomprehension of such places fuels one's present interest. When working, they are images of hell – noisy, smelly, dark – with suggestions of violence about to surface – mechanical thrashings felt through the rumbling ground, emissions of smoke like anger, sudden clangs like attacks.

For there is no other architectural discrepancy so vast – one's distaste for the working mill, one's fascination with its husk. Something like the violence the factory formerly contained within it will soon be directed against it; the mammoth has changed from aggressor to victim and now earns our wistful affection.

Ancient industrial buildings are almost a contradiction in terms, but when we find one, like the Arsenal at Pisa, it holds us in a special way. Much more unlikely than formal monuments, as if some things were built for eternity and others for the time being, so to save one of those, like all the unwanted tags which collectors of ephemera hang onto, is like an inversion of normal piety and perhaps an indirect discourtesy to it. It is much more remarkable for certain species to reach a certain age (than others), so the Arsenal is precious. And yet it is not, such a simple and featureless structure that it might be a set of nineteenth-century workshops.

You needn't know that Pisa cathedral is a cathedral to be amazed at it; until you're told the Arsenal is 450 years old you won't give it a second glance. But it shares many features you've come perversely to value in industrial structures: extreme monotony of form and material, the same

Industrial ruins have no antique dignity and are more vulnerable, awaiting possible demolition: New Brewery Yard, Burton.

arch repeated mindlessly, all in the same unvarying brick. And there are awkward joints left undisguised which a pompous building would cover or decorate. In industrial relics one gives these features meanings they don't have, as if Ledoux had done them, meaning by their dullness an individual's loneliness in the indifferent world, hinting thereby that life here is not fun.

Because they are so uncommunicative for long stretches, one attributes absolute integrity to industrial structures. When variety appears it will be purposeful, and will never exist for its own sake. Usually one doesn't understand what the corrugated eruptions on a brewery, say, are – those extensions like little gabled buildings which don't reach the ground. Unless you can smell the hops you don't even know it's a brewery, and so make up a little narrative of loading and unloading to explain idle bits which look as if they should be busy.

Seeing a lot of inactive sloping ducts or overhead walk-ways is an even greater spur to thought than if gravel rattles down them or indistinct workmen flit back and forth. Unused routes bring out the novelist in everyone, more than ever when one is sure, as here, that all linkages are urgent necessities in some sequence of refinement, conversion, or assembly.

The aesthete is seldom more credulous than when presented with brute facts of labour. However curious he becomes about the construction of an oil rig in the ocean say, he isn't likely to end up understanding why certain parts are painted blue and others orange, why pipes pass in front and not behind others, why some are richly stained and some, almost adjacent, remain pristine. The sight is so satisfying because it can't be questioned and must be as it is, for reasons more urgent than seemliness.

There is a kind of modern building which plays on this superstition that mechanisms are truer or more inevitable than art. Amazing to relate, this style has grown up in England, not the society of all others most at home with machines. Not so surprisingly perhaps, since Richard Rogers' buildings express a secretly picturesque view of technology. It gives one a way of including eccentric variety and even misrule in visions at the same time hard to fault for their rationality.

The most incongruous fact about the wilder hi-tech buildings is that they tend to be museums not factories, financial or cultural rather than industrial institutions. They are essentially gorgeous *pictures* of technology for those with sufficient leisure to interest themselves casually in workings. The technology is high not advanced (though it may be strange, a new way of doing something for which there is a cheaper, too-familiar alternative), but prominent. It is more visible, and there is more of it in proportion to everything else. As if, a nightmare, a cherished wish, life could be consumed or directed by it until nothing else was left.

The ideology of a structure like the new Lloyds insurance building in London – headquarters of an institution whose organization is as mysterious, and broken into non-joining parts as its envelope – is a notion of honesty in which the inside is shown as the outside, and services normally concealed are inflated and run outside them.

The effect though not the truth of this is that the walls have been peeled off to reveal, as in anatomical drawings, the grisly facts within, which the organism is ordinarily happy to forget and leave to unconscious operation.

Rogers' buildings are among the most energetic of structures, as if the violence verging on cruelty of the stripping away continued into the present and before our eyes. The sight is more outrageous than anyone has quite said, our response something like a patient's on being told he has an awful disease.

High-tech buildings are marvellous but alienated objects, as even one's own body becomes from the minute one inspects its workings or

Richard Rogers' Lloyds building in London, is curiously evocative of a ruin, its service structures revealed deliberately as a ruin's might be by accident.

hears that it contains intruders in the form of tumours or virus. Although they gleam with untreated metal or shout with visceral colours, although they look newer than anything in their vicinity, these buildings are objects in early states of decomposition. They are the most elaborate mock-ruins ever built, so it is not surprising that the most graphic ones, Richard Rogers' most extreme productions, should produce almost nausea, as in someone forced to observe dangerous surgery.

They may succeed in part because the verbal professions associated with them and their real meaning, their components and their essential being, are radically, even diametrically different. Some have seen them as soulless, robotized super-modernity, but their true power is to make buildings primitive creatures again, monstrous beings whose nearest model in the historical past is probably a steel mill in full cry, devouring its meal of raw materials noisily, passionately, and occasionally belching or roaring its satisfaction at nature ruthlessly following a preordained course.

The bottle kilns of Staffordshire (*left*) were used in the manufacture of pottery. Having outlived their function, they are like Surrealist sculptures, giant bottles as big as houses. And Battersea Power Station, London (*right*) is so powerful as a symbol that no one can bear the thought of its being demolished.

Superhuman scale prompts, not discourages, anthropomorphism. The huge ducts of a blast furnace (through which go mainly gases not liquids) are more like the main arteries between the heart and lungs than are the slender pipes clinging to walls of ordinary houses. Perhaps the largest scales revert to organic rather than geometric ways of folding things together.

And yet this is just as often not so. Bottle kilns, now obsolete relics, have a simpler and softer shape than most industrial structures, a shape more familiar at another scale. One can never be entirely sure that one form has not influenced the way another turns out, but here the kiln is like a bottle, not in thrall to prejudice, but through clear analysis of functions. Combustion and cooking on the one hand and pouring and storing on the other don't sound like acts which would be satisfied by the same shape, yet in this case they are. The resemblance forces us to think about the disparate processes together, making us see the kiln as a portable bottle, set down in a residential street temporarily, but long enough to grow onto the adjoining building. Until we are left with a Magritte fish-woman, a monstrous presence out of key with the lace-

curtain life on which it has imposed itself. Such symbiosis of industry and life can be more radical than Piranesi's visions of great hunks of Roman wall or tomb imperfectly absorbed by a humble contemporary street, through the machine's lingering suggestions of physical power.

When Battersea Power Station still functioned and spewed steam and smoke across the heart of London, it sometimes seemed a monster who produced the weather, a self-alienated object whose main features, four chimneys, were pushed as far from each other as could be, like the legs of an upturned table or prongs of a huge letter, from an alphabet a sentence of which would be the end of us.

Occasionally one gets a glimpse of an entirely industrial world, among the warehouses of Shoreditch now more empty than full, like buildings congealed into solid rock, occupying acres with hardly a suggestion of enterable space. Or, almost the contrary of this, the Isle of Dogs, some of the most urban space in London but the least built upon. Until it became an Enterprise Zone, meaning prey to development, it was the Pompeii of London. Like the wastes of northern New Jersey it had been claimed by brick and soot and ancient machinery, yet not fully

The Isle of Dogs, London, sank into dereliction within thirty years of the docks being abandoned, remote yet near the city.

occupied. A few landmarks like McDougalls' flour mills with their vast, clumsy elevators stood out, like Pyramids in the Egyptian desert, visible from many sides because the only route on the Island was a slow loop which circled it completely, and because frailer industries had been ploughed into the soil.

Until lately it was a place abandoned to itself where shreds of life – a few shops, a gaudy chapel now full of auto parts, crescents of workers' dwellings like enlarged crazy paving – failed to coalesce, as if someone had dropped them off without staying to unpack them. Islanders its residents were called, and clung to their land which was extraordinary as only the most despised and forgotten places can be.

Old aerial photographs of London from the East which focus on the river create the strongest longing for what can be no more. The Surrey Docks and the Island fill the foreground, and smoke obscures the only parts of London which most people know. It displays a whole novel of Conrad in an instant, endlessly murky activity, visionary grasp of a city which was richly, necessarily dirty, such a city as, coming to earth now, one only finds here and there in unimproved bits of dockland, where battered 1930s flats look across to a soiled rice mill, a sluggish river, and patches of unbuilt marsh.

The coatings of soot on industrial buildings, or rather of dark unfathomable dirt which seems infinitely complicated, not a simple repeated deposit of the same particulate substance, this is historical by itself, a sensuous record of activity which makes even two identical warehouse-boxes in Chequer Street, Finsbury, seem rich carriers of the past, seem from the overshadowed little alley between them a whole bounded world of clues about the lost language of London. Indelible as it looks, one can often dissolve (with the right solvents and enough persistence) the ink in which this message is written, but then one has washed away what made the building special.

The walls Michelangelo frescoed became something else; builders have often provided nondescript surfaces on which the weather and men's activity then began to write. One could make a sad list of buildings turned from rich to poor by cleaning, which, like the wretched Land Registry in Lincoln's Inn Fields, like a dog who has lost its hair, having seen ruthlessly cleaned, one would now like to see demolished, the logical end of the process.

Cleaning old things of whatever description is more treacherous than currently allowed. Paintings provide a controversial instance. Exciting as it sometimes is, does one need or deserve the sensation that centuries-old objects are just-finished acts? There are the ruins which speak of oft repeated activity, like highways which have been travelled any number of times. And there are the special cases which one knows have barely been used or used only once, like the giant portable harbours built for the invasion of Normandy in 1944 and now left near their intended anchorage, exposing more and more of their workings to view as the sea eats through the metal skin to show the structure beneath.

These are not purposeful memorials, just too expensive to move, which is also the case with the strangest one-use ruins of all, the Apollo launching sites in Florida. Again their poignance is that they sum up so little history, like a painting not overprotected by varnish but left outside in the rain from the day of its completion. We are astonished that anything so advanced and so thoroughly un-worn-out can look so discarded, as if through some acceleration which left it circling in empty space outside all human memory.

These objects, special enough to be unrecognizable, are on such more than human scale that keeping them in repair, supposing one had a

Apollo launching site, Florida, disused after having served its purpose once.

motive to do it, would be a Herculean task. But the sites look like places no one is ever going to see, littered with devices dropped by inhabitants in hasty flight. From afar one hallucinates that the largest erect structure is a Roman triumphal arch, surrounded by a desolation like no other, as if this bit of Florida had picked up its flavour from the places to which these vehicles are sent, as if the informing vision had created, before actually ascending into it, inter-stellar space on earth. In that perspective the most advanced technology always lies under threat of instantaneous ruin anyway, for it inhabits a spot where perfectionism and the litter-mentality meet.

CHAPTER V

Paintings

IT IS ALMOST inevitable that, in trying to extend the range of non-functional considerations in architecture, one should eventually turn to the avowedly fictional spaces in paintings. Even the soberest historian of architecture has probably been drawn toward painting when accounting for strong picturesque impulses in architectural styles like Baroque and Rococo. But apart from these isolated moments when paintings become architectural and buildings pictorial, the solider of these two spatial arts has an unfulfilled need of the other.

In paintings one finds spatial preferences expressed with an ideological purity architects can't really afford. Certain crises in the history of perception occur more explicitly in painting before spilling over into architecture. It is easiest to see the symbiotic relation between the picturesque and mechanistic views of reality which have warred for human allegiance over the last couple of centuries by tracing their first eruptions in painted form.

Painting is a truer inspirer of architecture when conceiving its own spaces architecturally, making flat surfaces which look built, than when it produces mock-ups of fantastic constructions, like the frothy super-Gothic we find in the background of many northern religious subjects. There have been painters like architects manqué, who express human relations as sets of spaces and volumes. Perhaps the ultimate test of the examples which follow would be to displace them into architecture proper, and to say what buildings they correspond to, not the type but the individual. Yet one turns to painting because it isn't making practical or even anti-practical proposals, as everything which puts itself forward as architecture is.

It seems appropriate therefore to start with a counter-example, an anti-architectural use of space. Hieratic images can offer useful provocation to the practical minds of architects, which are always looking for ways of bringing spaces into multivalent existence. Byzantine Madonnas, kept alive in Siena, are a type of the image as a single all-consuming place, which chokes on the richness of its filling. Thus many would see them as surfaces in which there is no space. But they are different from pattern by itself, from a certain length of brocade treated as a focus for our attention. For, although there aren't intermissions in the Madonnas, they are fiercely hierarchical, all other areas, even Christ himself, expressed as dependencies of the mother's face and hands. Brocade is ignorantly frontal, but Byzantine figures are frontal by choice. They are enthroned, the gable of the picture frame echoing the throne's pointed top, and making an expanding aura of presence.

These paintings provide a nest or resting place for the viewer who takes on a role like the Christ child, not intimidated but subordinated by the encircling presence. Sometimes the throne is circular and portrays thus her power to draw the surrounding space up into herself.

It is a profoundly anti-rational understanding of the physical world, that there are nodes of significance toward which all of reality rushes, becoming stilled and fixated when it nears the much desired goal. That this isn't mainly a matter of one's beliefs but a property imparted by certain forms of organization is shown by how stunned non-believers will become if they allow themselves to stare at these images. The experience is a kind of homecoming. One feels one has wanted the world arranged in the spreading ripple pattern without knowing to ask for it, as if everything were the rich folds of a welcoming woman's clothes, whose magnificence is measured by the ranks of tiny fleas in angel-form which hover at the edges of her garments. Primal or infant vision distorts sizes this way, like large discrepancies in the volume of rooms, and then at some point reason enters to equalize them and make all beings or spaces similarly real.

Among images that inculcate awe rather than rational comprehension there is a type antithetical to the hieratic Madonnas, or to the giant saints flanked by scenes from their lives like side corridors lined with monkish cells. The carpet-pages of the Lindisfarne Gospels are anti-focal; Byzantine devotional pictures maniacally centralized. The Lindisfarne organization is sub-democratic, a planned confusion, in which four aquatic birds have grown together, their necks twined like grape tendrils since birth and filling the entire space allotted to them in an uncontentious way. If one is interested, the circuit is colour-coded to make tracing the separate elements easier: necks are blue or green and go on forever, associating themselves with different bodies than their own. Wings are red-purple, talons grey, and at the other extremity of the creature, crest trailers are also, perversely, grey.

Left: Madonna and Child in the Byzantine style by the 13th century Italian painter Coppo di Marcovaldo. *Above:* Carpet page from the Lindisfarne Gospels, early 8th century.

These strange and subhuman spaces may give one the measure of more human ones, as if their aim was to be uninhabitable or to suggest a constant restless flicker of the eyes, or a mind unable to light anywhere, energy which exists by virtue of being unable to settle in a home. Or are they, all these cancelled routes, relaxed forays from a secure base like lush annual growth from a perennial root-stock? Instead, the play feels seized-up, frozen into permanence or architecture of unusable dimensions. Romanesque webs like this are anti-architectural, expending their ingenuity to crowd the chosen place out of existence, making it a nowhere with room for nobody. Despite their exuberance they are a type of negative act, and close every avenue, like rooms so small or crowded one can't enter them but only know of them, or count them while passing their entrances.

The Renaissance means, among other things, the widespread intrusion of an architectural mentality in painting. Subjects begin to be

The Last Supper in the Romanesque abbey of Pomposa, Italy.

conceived in three dimensions, as if the painting is only the model of a possible construction. So one finds depictions like the Last Supper in the refectory at Pomposa, which could, if anyone had thought to call on it, have made a contribution to the Renaissance debate on central-plan buildings. It shows a version of the circular space later to occupy Bramante, Michelangelo, and others, as a radially organized set of existences. Thus it narrates or populates an architectural idea, but more probingly than those topographical views of people in church interiors. In those cases architectural detail seems to interfere with spatial thinking, to close the questions which a generalized statement like the Pomposa table-full keeps open. And yet – such is its pivotal position – this can almost be read as two flat rows, like one of the old Romanesque diagrams, which treats a group of saints as a visual list along which the eye travels in series.

The introduction of perspective systems for giving illusions of depth extends architects' as well as painters' horizons, almost by itself makes new architectural forms possible. But it isn't a neutral tool, and in the hands of a secret backslider like Giovanni di Paolo finds itself pulled

The Birth of John the Baptist by Giovanni di Paolo.

aside into a Kafka vision, of recession which appears endless because dissected into crowded stages, tiered as well as recessive, making a space like a pile of boxes. In his *Birth of the Baptist* reality recedes independently in a number of different directions. The same cone-solid, which has come to represent the way reality takes its leave of our eye, appears as the bare floor between here and the other side of the room, *and* as the fireplace hood at right angles to it.

It is as if the cone-pointed-away-from-us has become a general emblem of the eye's coverage, which can now be seen as a detached form participating in various situations, a heraldry of optics. This is like being able to summon little replicas of the Baptist to show within the same picture later stages of his progress along a road. In both cases a centralized theory of perception has been treated decoratively, as if it made only richness and not unreality to multiply the number of complete worlds one commands.

There are some bizarre examples in Italian painting of perspective cones, often inverted, treated as objects, like the tent-structure made by all the human actors in the Pollaiuolos' *Saint Sebastian* in London. Here

Left: The Martyrdom of St Sebastian by Antonio and Piero Pollaiuolo. *Right: The Virgin and Child*, attributed to Robert Campin.

the lines of sight are drawn by archers firing arrows which come to rest, not neutrally, not unpainfully, in a human vanishing point, the saint's flesh. The primitive hut formed by this cooperative pyramid of bodies sits in a denuded landscape dotted with sophisticated but ruined structures and elegant little military parties, who are so far away the place is an ideal nowhere, abstract like a desert or the page of a mathematical treatise. So it is not a picture of suffering but of focusing, spatial rather than sensational.

There is really no Italian equivalent of the crowded Northern interior, wonderfully instanced by a few works attributed to 'Campin', the Virgin in a room much too small for her (stupidly enlarged by later restorers) where she appears to sit on the floor, or Joseph in his carpenter's shop, turning out mousetraps (snares for the devil or for innocent souls?). These rooms are all mousetraps, focusing the vision unconscionably, as if the best attention became immediately microscopic, as if miniatures not monuments were the model for important truths.

Italian intentness takes a different form and lures us to close inspection not of the whole picture surface pored over inch by inch, but of weird pockets into which we find ourselves drawn. Piero's *Flagellation*, a baffling work by a clearheaded painter, isn't exactly an interior but the abstract scheme ·of one. Like Aertsen's kitchens full of enormous vegetables and flayed carcases, with a tiny peephole onto the 'real' subject – Christ entertained by Mary and Martha – it inverts the apparent importance and the real interest of what it shows, as if, as often happens in daily life, if not in art, we are not granted a place near what we feel most affinity for or curiosity in, but off to one side far enough to miss the conversation, yet near enough to know it is taking place. Piero achieves the feeling of cramped space by means entirely different from Campin's, by disproportion not crowding, but the outcome for the viewer is similarly an act of decipherment following on spatial discomfort.

He is much given to mathematical conversions of one set of human figures or one part of the picture into others, which usually involves great disparity between foreground and distance. In the *Flagellation* it feels like a betrayal of the truth, unless normal meanings are reversed and foreground (the large figures to the right) means hardheartedness, and recession (a minute Christ in the left distance) means solemnity. Here Piero experiments with the emotional valency of various recessions, and

Piero della Francesca: *The Flagellation.*

Paolo Uccello: *The Hunt.*

as usual reaches ambiguous conclusions. The picture reads two different ways, laterally and recessionally, and yields two different answers, though one of these seems dramatically less valid. As a *pattern* it is pure but callous, as if seen by an unfeeling onlooker; as a *space* more profound, yet ragged, and disquieting. Piero defeats our need to know what to feel about these events or to find the meanings we expect. His unflinching reticence produces individual figures like radiant uncommunicative stones, making meaning like a building not a personal entanglement.

One could construct a series of paintings based on human colonnades, which is to say people converted to regular punctuation of the picture surface as in many Pieros. The Uccello *Hunt* in Oxford is a negative of this idea, which treats the picture space as an endless columned building, like the disembodying power of perspective, operating here as a black hole which evacuates reality. Trees equal columns, and the murky Gothic forest pushes the Renaissance spatial idea over some edge to become an anti-idea. Here is a vanishing point into which everything vanishes. It is one of the most convincing approaches to anti-matter ever presented: all this unified information exists in order to disappear. In spite of himself Uccello is pushed by science towards various annihilations, battles which dismember space, hunts which cancel it, always a form of active contest ending in destruction, a clear black vision.

The next phase of Renaissance spatial thought is neither so materialist nor so heroically pessimistic. Pontormo's spaces are more complicated and tentative, queasy not desperate, contradictory not meaningless. His

Story of Joseph is a surface missing its middle, where a crevasse has opened up leaving stranded cliffs on either side. It is a severed whole which is also folded back on itself: the same figure appears kneeling at the left, and mounting a stair on the right (twice). Space and time form confused parallel ridges like rumpled fabric. Anomalies and archaisms multiply, but here they always *mean* something and give the painter a mode for expressing his pervasive dissatisfaction. Cutaway walls and perched rooms aren't the innocent conveniences they would have been in medieval manuscripts, but uneasy advertisements that no one feels at home, and all existence is precarious.

Here no continuous movements are possible, and gaps appear in the ascending series, leading us forcefully away from thinking in fixed images towards sequences and developments, which are then disrupted and unpredictable. It is one of the first works where the mode of telling swamps the story, and the narrator's not the actors' problems absorb us –

Jacopo da Pontormo: *The Story of Joseph.*

Left: Stanley Spencer's *Christ Carrying the Cross.*
Right: Augustus and the Sybil by Antoine Caron.

a deflection onto the encasing structure rather than whatever lives might be lived in it. Which is how Pontormo can seem both nervous and numb, hyperactive and inert: he manipulates his personages heartlessly in order to bring the tumult in his breast to an end. All the intricacy hopes to find the means of sweeping itself away.

The tumult in some of Stanley Spencer's early paintings is more violent but more plausible. Objects are blown every which way as if by a prevailing wind. Or so we might think if we weren't used to the world in a quieter state. So it seems more likely that it is Spencer's vision, not blustery weather, which makes chairs careen and empty clothes billow up with a life of their own. People join or are dragged into these wave movements, swaying like grass or banging into each other when two impulsions collide. Pontormo, not any early twentieth century painter, is Stanley Spencer's nearest contemporary, but as he develops Spencer becomes less strange and more archaic, moving from Mannerist intensity to Gothic flatness.

In the crudest terms Spencer's development is from movement to pattern, from canvases in which strange configurations express tangled emotions to ones in which an arrangement expresses an arrangement. He moves from being a natural Mannerist to being a formal one, but oddly enough the monstrous objects which fight for the space with the figures – giant tea urns, post bags, or fluffy towels, moneychangers'

tables, Veronica's napkin, dead soldiers' grave markers – do not take over the space from people as he begins to find the life force less urgent. It isn't that the world petrifies into fittings: people themselves become fittings to the later Spencer, having some of the properties of inanimate things, hardness, smoothness, and powerful surface pattern. If we hadn't seen the earlier explosive and vulnerable Spencer we might think that these later works were more eccentric than we do, the works of a man who saw all of reality as a machine, the English Leger.

Certainly one of the mysteries of his career is how he remained so impervious to Continental influence, but maybe the price of this insularity was high, and being unable to admit certain kinds of stimulus meant that he was driven to a kind of self imitation like mass production. He had always had a quasi-architectural attitude to creatures, but at some point the tension went out of the conflict, and everything turned to stone.

One wishes he could have turned for inspiration to works like Antoine Caron's *Augustus and the Sybil*. This sixteenth-century de Chirico shows Rome as a population of monuments, which are individualized to the point of gawkiness so that they usurp the roles of human beings, who are happy to be relieved of responsibilities, to be passive-ized. It is a more purposeful vision of a mechanized world, all built, yet not dead or uneventful, because each finicky little column, arch, or rotunda is busy with miniature incident and far enough from the nearest others to depict estrangement which there is still hope of patching up, like a room whose diverse scattering of occupants is about to find some common ground.

One of the strengths of these earlier visions is that they haven't quite formulated themselves as a code: Caron still threads a venerable narrative through the monuments. He hasn't specialized to a painter of scenery pure and simple. Yet maybe his difference from the falsely animated late Spencer lies in not pretending to energy he doesn't have. For his inertia he finds the analogue of the field of monuments, whereas the drop in intensity is accompanied in Stanley Spencer by a more hectic surface commotion, among larger crowds whose members have lost their former distinctness.

So there is a kind of truth in Mannerist artifice, like that by which the miniaturist Clovio trades the picture for the border, until the vigour goes into the twisting figures of the frame, and the central scene shrinks into a little cameo whose actors are less distinct than the nudes writhing at its edge. These tiny stretches of vellum are like a set of Sistine ceilings bound between covers, small even by the standards of other books.

Clovio rejoices in limitations on his freedom. Given pages instead of walls to fill, he will make them mockeries of rarity, a tiny fictional treasury where the artificial has almost completely ousted the natural. Something similar has taken place in Patenier's landscapes, where the mountains are architecture in disguise. It is the perfection of the natural world to artifice. The whole surface will become an extensive precious stone, and trees or hermits will be small discolorations or imperfections which tell one something unimportant about the genesis of the jewel they cling to or have got mixed with.

In Mantegna and certain North Italian artists who resemble him the preference for stone has acquired a historical coloration – for everything to share mineral striations and to be organized inflexibly across common sense boundaries of objects is for our era to be classical, to remember in its substance, and thus to relive, Rome in the great days. An architectural grain in reality is the truest sign of permanence. Paintings become less ephemeral through a painted resemblance to stone.

When Mantegna shows Dido before her pyre, the wood which will obliterate her draws our eye away from the person. It is presented as a complex collection of different grades and species of timber, from twigs to logs, all carefully sorted. As he sometimes does, the painter has given a fictitious consistency to all this variety: everything including poor Dido is represented as gilded porphyry, preciousness with an overlaid, more

Giulio Clovio's *Adoration of the Shepherds*.

Dido by Andrea Mantegna.

exquisite coating of preciousness, a hardness analogous to unfeeling wood, but different.

By comparison with Crivelli, there is a kind of naturalism or scrupulosity in this. Crivelli's root principle is to turn every inch of reality to rock or crystal structure. No 'natural' explanation is provided (like Mantegna's that the canvas is really a carved panel or frieze, fragment of a larger edifice). Crivelli's way of accounting for his hardness of surface and brittleness of line is simply to make it compelling. Novelties can be fascinating *as* novelties, not because they uncover essential truth about reality. And this is how Crivelli's extravagances work, not to suggest an architectural framework subsisting below the surface, but to make surface everything. So his paintings cause a big rush of excitement which wanes as one gets used to

Marcus Gheeraerts: *Sir
Thomas Lee in Irish costume.*

them and figures out that everything is just raised one degree of
hardness. Flesh becomes tough skinned fruit, fruit becomes rock, cloth
becomes metal, marble becomes . . . a painted rainbow. The magic is too
evident, so the transformations seem mechanical.

Objectifying reality this way is architectural in a trivial sense, like
certain derivatives of Cubism which made society portraits into sleek
metal constructions. The Elizabethan version of the meeting of human
artifice and the natural world is less formulaic than Crivelli's. On the
rare occasions when Elizabethan portraits are set outdoors they present
the stander as a force of nature, the allegorical companion of woods or
water. Military ones seem far from the experience of battle, so that one
mistakes the gear of an Irish bog soldier for the dishevelled elegance of
masque costume. These woods are claustrophobic like a room, with
narrow corridors leading to preordained encounters, or to shields
dangling from trees, at the feet of which rest dragons like jewelled
pendants.

Marcus Gheeraerts: *Queen Elizabeth I*, the Ditchley portrait.

The pinnacle of such visions is the queen, who appears in the Ditchley portrait as England itself, an emanation from it more extensive than it, standing on a map of it, with the weather of the upper air flashing round her like further layers of her clothes.

These play a peculiar role in images of this era. Elizabeth's dresses form Blakean auras round her person, spreading her power beyond her own boundaries. The clothes seem usurpers of human functions, more powerful than the person, burying it in an unwieldy Crystal Palace, a non-organic form which swallows up the little stick insect of the human frame.

In the Gower portrait on the other hand, wider suggestions are less boundless. The world is admitted through two little pictures or windows which frame the queen in contrasting views, like sun and moon, or war and peace. They are one-second glimpses of a special kind of space which gained new force in this period, the museum or housed collection, which is a resting place or focus of rarities. What the queen is in the world of government, the museum is in the world of learning, the coincidence of all lines of sight or inquiry, a luxurious concentration of animal, vegetable, and mineral; of industry, art, and nature; of scientific instruments, paintings on unusual surfaces, and toys in exotic materials enshrining inordinate amounts of the carver's labour.

From this time forward museums of one kind or another have been a European obsession, so that they must often seem one of the identifying marks of that culture to outsiders. But never again have the spaces themselves in which museums are housed carried quite such magical force, so that they came to be depicted in a number of paintings which one now finds hung in museums, smaller museums within the larger, which set one thinking along a regress like the person on the cereal box one reaches for, who reaches for a box, on which another reaches . . . until a box is reached too small for the eye or the printing process to distinguish any detail at all.

One looks into a little box in which people are shown doing what one must perforce be doing at that very moment oneself – self-consciously contemplating an object in a special place set aside for the act.

'Museums' in these paintings are more active than ours, are in fact their ancestors, at a moment before they began to pride themselves on inflexible permanence. The paintings show museums in the course of assembly and collectors in the act of collecting, though the collection is finished in the sense that, if a few things are as yet unclassified or unhung, there is hardly room for additional finds. That of course is one of the possible economies of such places, that new acquisitions will always oust former ones. But we don't look at plethoric spaces thinking how we will upgrade them; rather we find elsewhere an object we want, and then solve the problem of where to put it.

The pictures differ from our museums even more in variety than in density. The walls are a mosaic of paintings arranged in a characteristically disjointed way – narratives, landscapes, seascapes, portraits, and still-lives put together innocently, with no attempt to form analytic sequences or close comparisons, because one thinks of the whole collection ahead of its parts, as if one is composing a single design like a great geometrical figure. The seventeenth-century collector is still more like a designer than a scientist (even seventeenth-century scientists seem to us more artists than scientists).

For us these pictures remain unsatisfactory works of art because of a quirk of scale. The collection, but not the painting, is focused on the sense of the whole. The painting signals the intrusion of a quasi-scientific outlook, which begins to lose track of the wood wandering among the

Connoisseurs examining works of art in a gallery, an anonymous Flemish painting of the 17th century.

trees, for both the charm and frustration of these works is their minuteness. Paintings on these walls are never represented as blurs, though speaking realistically we could not bring them into clear focus at the distance we are supposed to view them from. Here our vision is unorganically accurate, like laborious knowledge, not rapturous perception.

Likewise the inventory of the minutiae which fill table tops, cupboards, shelves. Most of these items are ridiculously small, not for the miniature people who ogle them inside the picture, but for us who are magically able to distinguish each one, though if our gross hands approached them we would immediately crush them. The perfection of these visions is based on rigorous barriers to our participation – such tininess is a form of alienation.

Working against this property of such a multitude presented so clearly is the liberating potential of the picture's wealth of reference.

Paintings are joined by sculpture, gold and silver utensils, coral, crystal, and jewellery, clocks and other scientific appliances, coins, insects, drawings, maps, books, carpets, and weapons, each of which is like a department ramifying into whole corridors or labyrinths of rooms, if, that is, one could escape the cold method of depiction.

This possibility in the old jumbled museum is presented even more forcefully by a painting like Elsheimer's *Minerva* in the Fitzwilliam, which is also tiny, as the Northern museum obsession demands, but totally obscure. Looking at it is like coming into a darkened chamber from noonday sun. At first one can't see anything at all, and then begins to make out the artist and model against a rich figured background, then the reader of a huge book by feeble candlelight, then the student of a murky globe, and maybe last Minerva herself who sleeps or perhaps meditates – all of it forming a catalogue of exploratory activities like our own, in an oracular space like Plato's cave, which without departing from the beloved Northern minuteness gives a powerful impression of the privacy of all perception and the insulation of one perceiver from another, whether they inhabit the same space or not.

Elsheimer has succeeded in conveying what a museum like those prosaically presented in the Flemish cabinet pictures *feels like*, without slipping into detectable unreality. They represent, above all, discontinuity of experience or perception, which looks like fragmentation in the

Left: Adam Elsheimer's *Minerva.*
Right: Andrea Odini with some
of the sculpture from his
collection, by Lorenzo Lotto.

prosaic views, and near-solipsism in Elsheimer. A museum or collection does, after all, his evocative vision reminds us, correspond to a crisis in the European world view. Serious collectors are picking up the pieces of a world they perceive, however dimly, however half-consciously, in ruins. One misses something important if one regards collecting as a cure for boredom or a luxury of leisure, because it always begins in deep feelings of imperfection.

The Italian way of presenting collectors and collecting is generally less comprehensive, the Italian approach to painting less subdivided. Thus Lotto shows Andrea Odoni among some of the best fragments from his collection of antique sculpture, but this is by no means all this art-lover owned. Though the dandyish little figures wandering among the collections in the Flemish art-closets are more jewel-like and hence nearer to objects in the collection, Lotto's sitter is more seriously confused with his prizes, which are nearer lifesize, consistently human in subject and consequently impinge more on the viewer's emotions. The scene is more than ever the aftermath rather than the heyday of civilization. Though the remnants are extremely precious they are beginning to look lifeless, which is their fascination, for we experience a morbid intensity among all these incomplete suggestions like unfinished utterances or involvements broken off before they can develop. This picture shows post-creative man brooding among the half-vanished

Gerrit Dou: *The Poulterer's Shop.*

efforts of others, sophisticated and paralyzed, who if he ever builds anything himself, as opposed to obscuring the lines of existing structures with accumulated furnishings, will construct small quarters of self-defeating complexity.

The later Dutch attitude to still life sometimes seems a descendant of the explanatory museum pictures. The heap or treasury is naturalized and brought nearer to ordinary necessities, though an outlet is left for art-obsession: elaborate appliances of the table; and for fruits of travel to exotic lands: non-native foods and dishes. There is a minor genre which intervenes briefly between the connoisseur's cabinet and the opulent table. It is a room stuffed with edibles not paintings, presented even more peepholishly than the telescopic inventories at the art-dealer's. The most interesting practitioner is Gerrit Dou who paints poulterers' shops or fishmongers' where some of the vividest items threaten to overflow the frame created by an open window into which we look. Eels slither from the grasp of the older woman leaning toward us, a scrawny bird pokes its head between the bars of its cage toward a few grains of corn. The room we're looking into is a little prison like the wicker cage; the most dynamic suggestion the painting can make is that we might be able to buy something from it. The items depicted are in a new sense for sale: the painting is a pouch or purse from which the contents could escape or find themselves purloined. That is how we can explain the fever of inspection such pictures incite; they set afoot a contest for possession and give us the rarefied pleasures of trespassers.

One of the greatest Dutch painters of this period also paints bounded boxes of private space, but our inspection of these is more disinterested: in Vermeer individual objects are analyzed to reveal unexpected structure. No wonder he is a twentieth-century favourite: no other painter before Cubism has so drastically re-composed the world at a molecular level, so that simple appliances of daily life become architectural conceits needing study to be properly understood.

There are those who doubt that Vermeer's is a structural inquiry, who suppose that the prominent faceting stands only for effects of light, and that the painter was possessed by a maniacal fixation on certain kinds of reflection, on sparkles above all. Others assume that these flickering sensations provided by the natural world are only pretexts for a thoroughgoing de- and re-composition of our knowledge, so that the final result is more like Lutyens than a photograph, a wilful stylization of sense experience which reduces it to a countable number of categories and creates arrangements of these which have more in common with

Jan Vermeer: *Woman in blue reading a letter.*

periodic sentences than untutored vision. Which is only to say that Vermeer drives sense experience *toward* abstraction, toward unrecognizability, and that we value him for his estrangement from unthinking, well-understood eyesight. He makes problems where there were none, multitude where there was one, articulation in featureless surfaces. Maybe it is not the only or the highest conception of art, and it seems nearer to architecture than painting, which is not always anxious to let us see how the world is put together. But by now no one argues any longer about the great satisfaction offered by an art of decomposition, showing how things work or at the very least how the mind goes about unravelling them.

In part it is as helpless participants in the twentieth century that we turn toward decomposed compositions. Inevitably works struggling against centrifugal forces or inharmonious urges in themselves seem the most moving or heroic to us. People differ about where it all began and about why such attitudes should prevail in the scene on which we find ourselves. But almost no one says that isn't how it is now.

A common culprit is the self-alienation or cross-examination that Protestantism arose to express or encourage. Many telling images exist which allow words and texts to usurp the place of pictures, flattening space in a way which would prove disastrous in the end for both painting and architecture. One of these shows Edward VI enthroned next to Henry VIII (his father's) deathbed, and sitting on top of the Pope's downfall, which occurs below.

It isn't fair to set such ill-mannered propaganda against the decorous displays of art-treasures from across the Channel, like comparing a limerick to a lyric. At its highest – in Hogarth say – the limerick mentality produces a rowdy richness beyond the powers of the anatomists of aristocratic collections. One might even say that the more polemical works are only taking seriously the mental fragmentation implicit in the assemblage of whole galleries of art-thing, far more than one can comfortably look at or unaffectedly enjoy, which therefore come to seem one's bulwarks against something they form a wall to exclude.

Panel paintings and most sizes of canvas seem intended for more intimate conditions than these large halls crammed with their smallness. When the museum exceeded a certain size, it became a perversion of the nature of its parts, and gave further impetus to disintegrative tendencies in the perception of space and of man's location in the universe. Being encyclopedic had always entailed a risk of being incoherent: from a certain moment in the sixteenth century in Europe, alert perception of

A Tudor allegory of the Reformation, showing Edward VI enthroned, with Henry VIII on his deathbed, the Pope collapsing, Protestant clergy round a table and (through the window) the destruction of images.

whatever dimensions seemed to partake of these deficiencies, which lends most products since a mournful, Romantic intensity.

A fragmentation of mind which had its origin in plethoric wealth of stimulus becomes in the end inseparable from almost any perception, of fields however confined. Even so alien and un-Protestant an artist as El Greco shares something with the broken vision of the picture of Edward VI, where discordant inscriptions jostle. Space in El Greco's *Expulsion of the Moneychangers* is more fluid and chaotic partly through the painter's greater skill: maybe the most expressive qualities of the Edward image are inadvertent. Discontinuity is more deeply imbedded in El Greco, and makes whorls and eddies in the structure of reality, as if to say that experience is uniformly spiritual, but incommunicable; as if, truly perceived, the universe is myriad realities physically adjacent, but, in the ways which really count, as remote from each other as the furthest stars.

So the connectedness of the world we see is an illusion the artist can make use of, and in any case no one could depict the underlying state of affairs in its nakedness. When El Greco focuses on a single figure he shows its parts at war with each other, the clothes fleeing from or trying to carry off the body, bits of decoration on it – such as a large embroidered cross – evaporating or burning a hole in the cloth, furniture in a state of rebellion of which no one can guarantee the outcome.

Religious *intensity* does not seem exactly the right name for this state of affairs, which is above all an exhilarating vision of conflict, of heresy as the motive force in matter. Ways of seeing and feeling multiply more quickly than they can be suppressed. The battle differs from other battles because all the warring positions are so deeply meant, because here variety isn't play but deadly and costly exuberance.

In compositions with many figures this vision is sometimes given more explicit character as a set of bubbles or storms, spatial convulsions creating room-crystals in which different perceivers are sealed up. Like many El Greco subjects *Gethsemane* is *about* the mutual incomprehension of different perceivers or dullards. In this case there may be an overarching pattern which knits up the different participants without their knowing and gives an unorthodox meaning to this long-familiar event.

In some sense the greatest proof that the sixteenth century witnessed a geologic shift in European spatial perception is the fact that artists as different as El Greco and Bruegel provide us with comparable instances of centrifugal organization. Among examples of dispersed structures, some of Bruegel's early paintings hold a special place. One like *Carnival and Lent* appears formless, anti-architectural, yet even before one discovers how, one senses it is not. Instead, the design is radically decentralized, consisting of many autonomous nodes, as if one has used the materials of ten paintings to make one. Later, Bruegel combines this mind-boggling individualization of the picture space with larger central cores, the most static of these being his depictions of the world's most imaginary building, *The Tower of Babel*.

That central focus seated stolidly in the middle of the picture seems to give him licence for the most extreme centrifugal tendencies in detail, the nearest thing to an infinite dishevelment of people and buildings radiating from their large point of origin. Even when he appears to offer monoliths, Bruegel is busy breaking them down by finding imperfections in how grand plans (or any plans) are carried out, more interested in lean-tos built against them than the walls towering out of sight, the kind of observer who ends up focused on individual bricks and finds them endlessly various. The world in a grain of sand, the history of mankind in the progress of a penny is realized with less falsehood or convenient ellipsis by Bruegel than any other painter.

Opposite above: El Greco's *Expulsion of the Moneychangers*
and (*below*) his *Gethsemane, the Agony in the Garden*.

Two paintings by Pieter Bruegel the Elder: *Battle between Carnival and Lent* and (*below*) his *Tower of Babel*.

Carel Fabritius: *View of Delft*.

Yet among the squandering of incident, of lives scattered like seeds rooting where they fall, subsists the sense of an underlying pattern that we lack the skill to read. The universe is a building which its inhabitants are too small to perceive, most of the time, as a single shape. This truth is sometimes more clearly presented, as in *Hunters in the Snow*, a wintry member in the series of months where bones of a landscape show through – tree trunks as dark columns on a snowy ground. Yet the various geometrical elements never gel except in the painter's mind – you can't make actual habitation from bare trees and frozen ponds. So the disorder in Bruegel usually feels more vivid than the order, which is notional.

He might have sympathized with later attempts to turn space inside out, like Carel Fabritius' little *View of Delft*. There the edges of vision are suddenly easy, and the centre unattainable, as if it fled away from us seeking non-existence. It may have been painted using a convex mirror, and some have thought it was made for one of those peepshows which created tiny illusions of architecture but which are otherwise inward, not outward looking. Fabritius' is a more daring spatial distortion than any other which has come to light, like the antibody of architecture, a vision of matter fallen so out of sympathy with the eye that it tries to avoid being in the place we are looking at.

The poignancy of this image of human self-alienation is its earlyness. Eventually one gets used to such absence, but even in Degas it is still potentially tragic, and still passed off as a study in optics. His more conspicuously radical works are blatantly partial views, a lady sprawled

Edgar Degas: *Ludovic Lepic and his daughters in the Place de la Concorde, Paris.*

on a sofa but seen through a painfully straitening doorway. Or someone seated in a dark room against a window which obliterates the surrounding reality by its aggressive effect on the focus of the eye. Degas is able to unite relaxations of technique which seem effrontery not freedom to some (but they are juvenile misbehaviour about as much as Japanese calligraphy is), together with Puritanical stringency which is like forcing reality creep through the eye of a needle.

The most wonderful Degas of all is now associated with Berlin, because it disappeared there in the war. It shows a piece of Parisian road surface carefully selected for inconsequence, as if after deliberating exquisitely over what paper to write on, a Japanese courtier had finally settled on the fine texture of cinders. This painting which includes by the way a portrait of a nobleman and his two small daughters is more like Berlin than Paris because the German city is for us a purer embodiment of the vacancy at the heart of the hubbub of cities, as if in certain intervals reality had fallen through into non-existence.

All these compositions of Degas show an urban world where eccentric uses of space create accidental intensities. For all their calculation, they are visionary glimpses flashing upon the retina with a sudden shock: the disproportion between the Vicomte Lepic and his

Piet Mondrian: *Dune V.*

two tiny daughters can never be put right, nor can one undo the
alarming disjunction in the ways they are facing or about to walk. Even
within the family, in its infancy, modern life exercises centrifugal force
and sends the unprepared members off in different directions like lonely
bits of an atom.

But it is a glimpse of motion frozen into structure, a persuasive
building made of the constantly repeated but ephemeral moment of
crossing the street. In some sense one cannot fix this crucial act, for traffic
arrested is no longer traffic. As do the Japanese works it makes one think
of, Degas records most faithfully the powerful desire that time should
stop – *that wish* is dependable and architectural.

Inspired of all things by grain elevators and factories, architecture in
the early twentieth century became more abstract, avoiding obvious
imagery in the form of ornament, and also giving up more important
signs by which buildings had signalled their purpose. The analogue in
painting of these attitudes is Mondrian, who appears to achieve *pure*
structure by concentrating on simple allotments and junctures in the
space to the exclusion of everything else. After many paintings
suggesting intimate domestic spaces, he came in the end to a series
(Broadway Boogie Woogie) resembling a street grid with jazzy

interruptions akin to the stops and starts of traffic and the constant noise of car horns.

It may not be the most reliable gauge of his later meanings, but tracing his development from tame Jugendstil landscapes to the later work provides interesting clues. The young Mondrian usually isolates a single object – church, sand dune, or gnarled tree – against a neutral ground, as if it's come indoors or been brought into the mind. He is then free to concentrate on complex form in isolation, as in a laboratory. It was the laboratory-air which finally soured the public on purist works of architecture like a series of hospitals, which hadn't been true to the squalor and improvisation of their industrial models.

In the same modernist vocabulary were works nearer to Monet than Mondrian, like Philip Johnson's own house and Mies's Barcelona pavilion, which used the minimalism of the style to produce aqueous or transparent effects, buildings which shimmered or even disappeared, whose sharp edges were not strong assertions but harbingers of invisibility. Perhaps it is a nebulous base for a school of architecture, but it would be fun to see what the pursuit of lilypond vagueness brought in the way of solid structures.

For of course even the most un-centred Monets are less boneless than they appear, though when new they argued for a loosened, disorganized view of the world, which purported to be more natural but depended on underlying grids all the same. To live up to the formal innovations of the water lilies, in architecture, we would need to find a way of disregarding the top–bottom orientation which controls so much of how buildings look (not to speak of how they are). And also to arrange a small number of emphases which just failed of symmetry, most disconcerting of all, neither clearly regular nor strongly irregular.

It sounds an abstract, unrooted programme for architecture, yet if the arts are to learn from each other, isn't it just the more recalcitrant discoveries in the sister art one should try to give form to? Where are buildings like the most compelling architectural effects in twentieth-century painting, Monet's endless ponds of wavering edge and uncertain depth, which transform plants into clouds and reflections into solid bodies? It would be an architecture of illusion, where if one identified the liquids and gases, as say glass and marble, one would be greatly surprised or confused. It would hardly look like building at all, but then, contrary to what is said nowadays, this is an important part of what this art has always been about, to provide exciting fictions and to show one objects known, even as one experiences them, as facts which cannot really be.

CHAPTER VI

Unbuildable Buildings

THERE ARE those who hold there are no unbuildable buildings, only unbuilt ones. But even if we leave aside gross infringers of gravitational or other natural law – like three mile unsupported bridge spans or office buildings taller than the atmosphere is thick – we have no trouble finding interesting designs which if built would be betrayed by the techniques used to erect them. Many unbuildable buildings of this sort have been built, and can be inspected, structures in which necessary joints obliterate some sweeping curve which was the whole point of the design. If one could afford to be exhaustive one would match up the drawings with the building in countless cases, and eventually accumulate a stock of examples which looked better on paper than when built.

That is really to sabotage the concept, which may not be as absolute as one wants to think. Perhaps one cannot separate true architectural impossibility from the social will to build. One could make a collection of unbuilt architects which would include designers as interesting as Friedrich Gilly, and how could one be sure that historical mischance hadn't played a large part in their nonexistence as architects?

No other art is vulnerable in a remotely similar way. *The Faerie Queene* and *The Canterbury Tales*, great examples of unbuilt, or half-built, literary works, are incomplete because their authors lacked time and will to finish them, not because they needed huge commitments from others which weren't forthcoming.

In no other art could one claim that there were two forms of architectures, plans on paper and structures in stone and brick. The nearest anyone has come in other arts is to claim that Rubens, Constable, or Picasso is more himself in rough sketches than in finished compositions, which is rooted in a Romantic idea that an artist's ideas are best when freshest, or most primitive, as infants or sketches.

Such ruinous ideology of the emergent work aside, we may still feel that an idea of the unbuildable which comes down to technical know-how or ignorance and no more is unpleasantly crass. Just as there are buildings which contrive to look more impossible than they are (Bohemian Gothic vaulting, the smallest building of Ledoux), there are many seeming plans which are intended as fictions, so that if one built the fantasies of the illustrator of *Hypnerotomachia*, in some sense not impossible, one would have something like the movie of the book. A garden populated with those particular monsters (of no great size) could rise no higher than an interesting misunderstanding.

On the pages of *Hypnerotomachia* these ideas preserve ambiguities it would be harder to incorporate in structures: a drawing's minimal linearity can be read as either elevation or plan, either a pyramid crowned by an obelisk, or a focusing passage with great voids on either side.

Partisans could probably be found who would argue that some of the most interesting actual structures are fictional in a related sense, pretending to infinite extent or perhaps just occupying more space than one can find any rational warrant for them to do. It is so common for certain types of enclosed space to be bigger than any conceivable crowd or set of activities which will ever occur there, that it is hardly thought of as a fiction. A law court or cathedral *without* a void at the centre would seem peculiar.

The occasional fictionality of real buildings shouldn't be separated even from such unpicturable architecture as that of Kafka sketches like 'Before the Law' and 'An Imperial Message'. We might even begin with all the buildings which can be thought but not pictured, like these centripetal or centrifugal infinities in Kafka's words. Are they only tricks of scale or of number? Surely there is more to impossibility than grandiosity or senseless multiplication.

Of all arts architecture is the one which consistently de-trivializes, though it can't de-relativize, scale. The size of the human organism doesn't have much bearing on literature or even on music. When we talk about a novel's size we mean its length, but a symphony fills space as well as time. More people than Erich Mendelsohn have experienced music as a series of structures, which grew and collapsed and reformed again according to a logic not available to an architect.

But the essential point for architecture is that the perceiver is a building already, that as well as the inhabitant he is an ideal rival of the contemplated structure matching himself against it not just to see how well it will fit him, but how well it measures him. The scale of certain Renaissance ideal designs means they remain a kind of child's play, but in Michael Graves' hands a set of tiny studies for a whole façade becomes successive stages, imparting a movement like that of thought to a

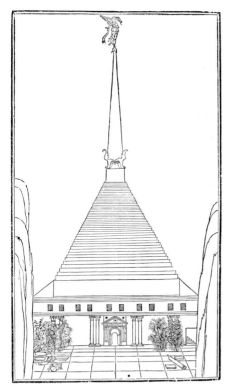

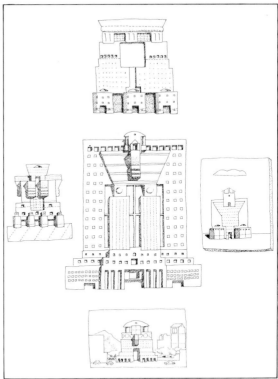

Left: Woodcut from *Hypnerotomachia Polifili,* 1499. *Right:* sketches by Michael Graves for the Portland Building, Portland, Oregon.

building. On his completed projects he sometimes makes a stab at capturing these changes like a rapidly developing life form, an effect dependent on the toy scales at which they are pictured, because such instantaneous grasp would be lost the minute you had to walk around or between them. The trouble is that these features are easiest to axe from the plan, because they remain symbolic structures, pictures of buildings even when shown in three dimensions. So the little collection meant for the top of the Portland Building fell by the wayside because someone didn't care or didn't realize that this gallery of characters like the cast of some yet-to-be-mounted play, held the key to Graves' design, a metamorphic sense of the life in forms, or an idiosyncratic idea of history which usually arrives stillborn when it travels from his sketches to his buildings.

The other place (besides the page) where the flux of invention often seems to continue into the spectator's present is in landscape gardens, also the only other scene where one can expect to find *small* architectural impossibilities. Buildings scattered or concealed like jewels in a perfected landscape may be episodes in a drama or variations on a single idea like the Graves search for the best face, resulting in a lively cartoon, which only makes practical decisions harder. Gardens are different because having it both ways is expected of them. There one can build a dozen competing versions of one's ideal residence, carapace, or goal; dissatisfied with the finality of buildings, architects and their clients find an impossible freedom to choose and not to choose in gardens.

They are places for the indecisive who prefer their facts virtual not actual, a vision which though permeating a whole landscape is broken into indistinguishable bits. Contrarily one reaches infinity in a single leap, with one engulfing image. Yet a surprising number of grandiose visions are dependent on concealed step by step narratives like journeys through a garden. Boullée, one of the most relentless fabricators of infinitudes, often gains his effect by specifying the separate grains of sand which make up his beach. Some would hold that an idea expressed only in perspectives isn't truly architectural, and perhaps Boullée inhabits some hinterland where the literary meets the visual.

His design for a Royal Library is one of the most telling. The sides of an enormous barrel vault, open at each end like a long section of sewer pipe, are lined with minute rows of books. Like a problem in calculus he breaks the simple space into a multitude of increments; the ceiling is similarly divided into lots of book-shaped coffers. So the spectator is coaxed to perceive eternity second by second, all the tiny human figures in the drawing slowing one's progress down the files. Then it strikes one that the space contains more experience even than the separate physicality of all its units. One imagines reading one of the books in this library, and realizes the integers here are not moments but lives, each of which could lead back into itself, stretching the experience of the whole library to impossible dimensions, immobilizing an imaginary reader in front of every book.

There is some pretence here of practical space, though the books which dwarf us are dwarfed in turn by the empty vault. Boullée's Monument to Newton is more perfect, because it successfully defies any attempt to use it; it is the most magnificent unusable space ever imagined, a dome with its literal-minded fulfilment underfoot, in a second answering dome. To conceive this proposal as two hemispheric domes may seem a lengthy approach to the fact that it is simply a hollow sphere on a heavy base, a base which disappears when one goes inside. Simple as the form may be in some sense, the building is sophisticated. Architectural precedents are to be found among domes, and as a

Two visionary designs by Etiènne-Louis Boullée. *Above:* Royal Library. *Below:* Monument to Sir Isaac Newton.

building project it comes apart into stages. It has even been suggested (a more knowledgeable view than mine) that the most refined pleasure produced by this project is the idea of the scaffolding which would be required to build it. Perhaps the fact he didn't provide drawings of that machinery shows that Boullée's mind isn't very process-oriented, and that he wants perfection with belittling props removed.

For in this project he has taken on the job of representing the universe and done it better than reality and the naked eye had previously managed between them. The boldest stretch of his scientific ambition is its inversions. In the Newton monument day is night and night is day: small holes in the skin which let daylight in are perceived as stars by the spectator standing near the base of the sphere. At night when the stars are darkened an artificial source in its centre illuminates the whole closed universe. Without question Boullée hasn't troubled himself over how large the holes must be in order to be perceptible from the ground hundreds of feet below, or how much distortion in the heavenly pattern will occur because one can't let the holes overlap the joints between the panels the sphere is made of (masonry in Boullée's drawings, steel in the most likely modern projection).

The whole is perfection because all this constructive and engineering skill is deployed to create a single point of vantage for contemplating an even greater engineering work, the heavens. The 'building' consists of a small viewing platform (not quite a literal point) which focuses one on a powerful but bounded spatial experience. He makes our relation to architecture like our relation to the sky. Though detectably a human achievement it is almost entirely beyond us; as if to say Newton's great discoveries must remain incomprehensible to the mass of mankind.

To build a large dome was for centuries the height of most architects' ambitions. Perhaps the last to be denied it were Lutyens and Albert Speer, both in their different ways stopped by the last big war, after which skyscrapers not domes became firmly established as the form which overweening buildings must take.

Wren's first plans for the new St Paul's were much purer works of architecture than he was finally allowed to build. A centrally planned domed structure, the form he wanted, is more like a world than a building is usually allowed to be. One can glimpse even in the eighteen-foot Great Model, which is as far as he got with this idea (and after all far enough that some enthusiasts consider *that* miniature one of the best buildings of its century), how much more cosmic the dome he eventually built would seem if it rose above a symmetrical base like this. The sweeping concavity of the walls mysteriously answers the

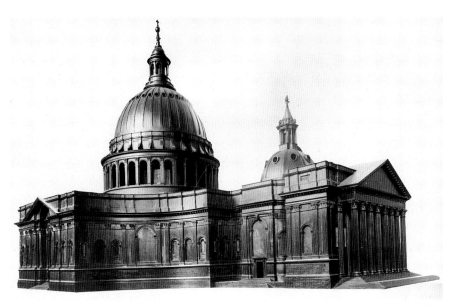

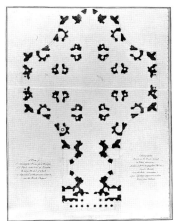

Plan and model (The Great Model) of an unbuilt centralized scheme for St Paul's, London, by Wren.

convexity of the dome, obverse and reverse of a single idea, the most compelling one in the classical repertoire.

Now domes are relegated to the scrap heap of crazy inventions. Contemporary instances are the province of someone like Buckminster Fuller and go up, only to come down, at World's Fairs and other great centres of frivolity like Epcot land in Florida. About a century after Wren an interesting signal was given of the shift in grandiose geometries from architects to engineers. Thomas Telford proposed, as a replacement for London Bridge, a single arch structure with a higher and more enveloping profile than any built there before or since.

The most telling view of it, taken from a rather low vantage, shows it enclosing the dome of St Paul's. Telford's bridge would dwarf the

Thomas Telford: scheme for a single-span London Bridge.

whole human world with an intimated circle, which exceeded the largest built one in sight, the dome which had naturally become a standard by which cultural facts were judged. Since Telford's time, bridges and road systems have stolen some of the grandeur of architecture and are now the biggest and boldest things man builds. Better than ordinary works of architecture they enshrine the meta-physical approach to technology, which sees it as a visionary medium for realizing the most far fetched dreams.

In one of its main modern efflorescences, visionary technology has shaded into personal expressionism, and so there have coexisted in the same designer, at least in different periods of his career, Utopian scientism and obscurantist strains implicitly anti-scientific. A number of twentieth-century German architects followed this two-stage develop-ment, passing from Romantic mysticism to rationalism and partway back again, in an abortive return journey near the end of their careers.

Most radical of the Expressionists, though he never built anything, was Hermann Finsterlin. His fantastic carbuncular studies are the most indivisible and obscure 'buildings' ever produced, and the most emphatically unbuildable. They take various forms – perspective drawings, clumsy models, plans. The perspectives are lightly flushed with colour like inflamed growths, almost-beautiful abscesses teeming with protuberances of organic shape, a blend of vegetable root and animal limb. They are labelled church, university or mausoleum almost indiscriminately, each filling a function with high symbolic content, but unspecifically. Trying to imagine how the space is divided internally one soon realizes one is barking up the wrong tree.

Clinching proof that these are consciously imaginary, comes when we meet a Finsterlin plan. They have exactly the same form as the perspectives, except that now a flourish becomes, instead of a decorative termination like a finial, a sliver-like room stranded at the end of a narrowing limb of them. The visions are not conflated, as is the rule in architectural drawing, where these two forms are mutually dependent and don't make complete sense in isolation.

Irresponsible as he undoubtedly is, Finsterlin pushes back the boundaries of architecture, not in the plans with their simple misunderstanding of picture for plan, but in silhouettes freer than most sculpture, starting from the other end entirely and wondering first of all what shape the building should be, allowing nothing to be dictated by what is easy to construct. So you end with no straight lines and nothing perpendicular to the earth. In fact, although Finsterlin's results look supremely organic, no actual organism is so lopsided or deviant – his

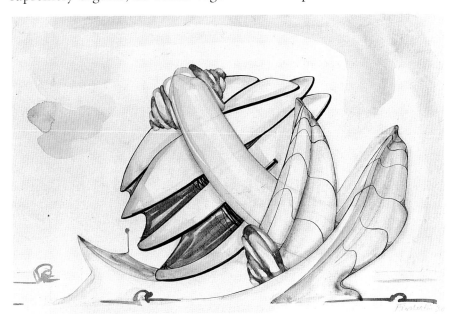

Fantasy building and plan by Hermann Finsterlin.

buildings are really parts or slices of organisms, or more accurately are like proliferant clumps of simple life-forms, bacteria, fungi, or algae. So even the most elegant look unhealthy and parasitical, excrescences not sane wholes.

To build them would require the most devious methods, which utterly betrayed their form, beginning with careful dissection, separate molding of each part, and inglorious bolting to re-arrive at the whole, a scenario which only confirms that they are among the purest paper-buildings ever devised.

Mendelsohn's famous sketches in reed pen – railway stations, factories, or cinemas on tiny scraps of paper like single Chinese characters – are actually much nearer to likelihood. Invariably he shows them turned on a diagonal to the spectator, partly concealing their symmetry, which is always lateral not longitudinal. Much of their novelty therefore lies in organization like a vehicle rather than a building. They appear to be speeding forward, or, no more plausibly, braking suddenly to the halt required of a large building.

It seems a shame to flatten the effervescence of all these racy ideas, but there is a humbling lesson in the fact that Mendelsohn built only one of them, turning increasingly thereafter to more rational programmes. Never mind that the Einstein tower is his most exciting building; it was almost bound to remain one of a kind, once everyone had realized how laborious and costly it was to obtain such glyphs of spontaneity.

Like the playful *jeux* he dashed off under harsh conditions at the Russian front, it is a well designed machine in rapid motion, with gorgeous thrusting and trailing edges, the latter especially subsiding in a complex series of curves. This most effective of architectural narratives is an exquisitely tailored event in time, with its beginning, middle and end, all of which is symbolically appropriate to its function of unravelling the history of the universe. The heavens appear static but are actually rushing on, and undergoing change as they move. Mendelsohn's tower conveys the excitement of a smattering of Einsteinian physics picked up from a scientist-friend. It is his homage to the instability of matter and its convertibility to energy, a reassertion of the history of objects over their physical density.

It is one thing to build a temple of scientific inquiry which takes great pains to embody such poetry, another to do it for a hat factory or department store. One could say that in deviating from the extravagant programme of the Einstein tower in the projects which followed it, Mendelsohn was only being true to the nature of the tasks he was successively set. Finsterlin's inflexibility, making every building a

Erich Mendelsohn: series of sketches for a factory and (*right*) the Einstein Tower, Potsdam.

monument to his own dreams, so that all functions look the same, appears in this perspective deeply inorganic.

Besides this, and perhaps more importantly, the experience of building the Einstein tower was a sobering one. Mendelsohn may have come away convinced such architecture wasn't feasible. Photographs taken during its construction show the building following a perverse route to its primitive goal, a single forceful image of motion. The base and cap are built of concrete as the forms lead one to expect. But in between is a large portion constructed of brick in clumsy approximation of the intended windswept form, which is then coated in elaborate rendering to achieve the final spontaneity. So the more one knows about the building's growth the more pictorial it becomes. Perhaps on the other hand knowledge of its complex hidden workings should lead one to respect it as one does the body which conceals the skeleton, whose exact form would be hard to derive from external clues.

Judging from photographs, however, one of the Tower's disappointments is the blandness of its internal spaces, which have been regularized to form the nearest possible approximations to the normal geometry of rooms. These are not organic cavities left over by intersection and crossing of bone and cartilage, or tunnels like living routes through the

Bruce Goff: the Harder House, built for a turkey-farmer in the form of a turkey.

building's substance, but cramped replicas of the straight edged spaces one arrives at when starting from an entirely different base.

It is easy to see why the building as a powerful image like this will not work. Why should there be any correspondence to speak of between symbolic depictions of a function and the spaces required to perform it? And in some sense the more effective and specific the symbolism the less legitimately repeatable in any future building. The purest architectural symbolists would start over from scratch with each new commission. There are a few architects who appear to do that. Of all structures, Bruce Goff's various works look least like each other. Perhaps this variety is a code which could be cracked, and one would see the same principle dependably repeated. The secret probably lies in the plans which are all radial – everything emanates from a number of nodes.

In the absence of this clear grasp of a controlling idea we find each design highly arbitrary, and it is this which causes them to look impossible, like the house in the form of a turkey built for a turkey farmer. It is clothed on its up-facing surfaces with bright orange carpet, as if it were trying to signal to other flying things, or were a boring old Howard Johnson's about to spring into life. Like most Goff designs it doesn't really lie still: all the corners of the roof turn up like a kite responsive to the wind, or like some weird Eastern import. The natural imagery – strong bird forms or walls trailing off into the soil like an eroded mound left by children on a beach – is filtered through popular culture and so feels impure. All these cacophonous influences add up to a soft, brash product, a little shocked at its own temerity. How did I get this way? it seems to ask.

On the surface they are impossible buildings. When one looks at them in detail, one finds them carefully built up in a series of small acts, crusted over with a multitude of discordant little inventions which are only not crazy because so patently sincere. The architect's conception of the clients' needs may at first be hardly recognizable to them, but it makes all the difference that his eccentricity is trying to serve them, and, by routes which seem at first strange, to give them what, until it appears like some monster from a dream, they have deeply wanted without knowing it.

Buildings looking like other things than buildings would be a rewarding class to collect. Lequeu's stable in a quiet meadow in the form of an enormous cow is one of the most outrageous. A house in the form of a bird you make your living by raising is one thing, a house for cows which looks like a cow is another, an advertisement which like many of its author's works might almost owe something to twentieth-century merchandizing.

Jean-Jaques Lequeu's stable in the form of a giant cow. Now considered a Duchamp spoof.

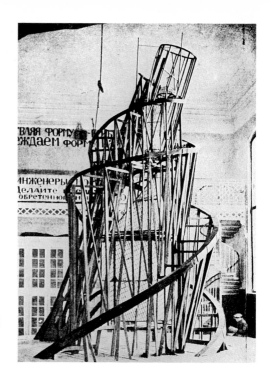

Right: 'Tatlin's Tower', the proposed
monument to the Third International
by Vladimir Tatlin, 1919. *Far right:*
N.A. Ladovsky's scheme for a block
of flats reminiscent of a crane, 1920.

Recently the idea has infiltrated academic consciousness that the
eighteenth-century crank Lequeu, one of the world's fringiest paper
architects, is really Marcel Duchamp inserting himself Trojan-horse-
like into the musty tomes of the Bibliothèque Nationale, whiling away
countless hours creating a large hollow space in which a few hundred
pseudo-eighteenth-century beings can roost.

If this is true, and this hoax actually took place, Lequeu's unbuilt
buildings are impossible in a way many have not realized. They couldn't
be built in the eighteenth century because they didn't exist then; they
can't be built now because so historical – so they inhabit a kind of limbo
in which they bump their heads on impossibility whichever way they
turn. Something is fishy about them as the products of M Lequeu, and
yet they have been believed for so long that they can't get out the back
way into the present, for their path is blocked by all that solidified
misapprehension. In the end they are works of both periods and neither,
shadows whose reality is obvious, whose meaning is permanently in
doubt.

There have been a few historical moments in which unbuildable
projects became almost a fashion or norm; the early Revolutionary
years in Russia are one. Conventions were inverted in another way as
well: the most despised building types were loaded with symbolic
prestige and so one got monuments or housing doing their best to look

like industrial buildings, workers faithfully constructing the new life, whimsies as pictorial in their furtive fashion as Lequeu's cow.

Tatlin's famous memorial leans to express its dynamic intention, violating old codes of beauty. It uses the ideology of machines – workings exposed and visibly working – living spaces here would have rotated at three different speeds – to frame abstract statements about the cosmos. It is an uproar turned toward eternity.

Less impressive and more transparent as a piece of thinking is Ladovsky's attempt to project a block of flats as the arm of an enormous crane, from the outward edge of which one really expects to see tackle hanging. Soviet architecture doesn't stand still or idle; in this case it is so eager to move forward it forgets that to make such motion permanent one needs to support it. It leaves out the considerable superstructure of wires along its top edge which is the only way one could preserve something like the outline proposed. All the symbolic practicality of the dwelling-factory was enough in the designer's eyes, blinding him to literal impracticality. Under the new code of ugliness and interesting disorder, very simple flaws slip in.

From houses like factories, to *factories* like factories, more like them than is really convenient in ordinary life, which is how they appear in the tireless studies of the belated Constructivist Chernikov. This series is one of the most curious comments on industrialization ever produced,

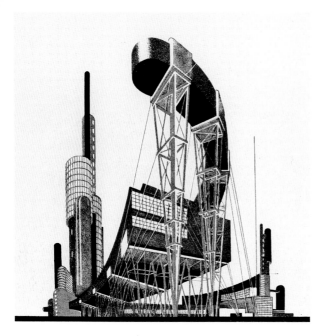

I. Chernikov: fantasy scheme for a
factory, one of an extensive series.

which turns it into pure picture. Some of the designs are supposed to
embody specific manufacturing process – airplanes, generators or steel
being produced in them – but most are plants in general, collections of
symbols or gestures along the skyline, cranes, ducts and walkways.

They emanate from the strenuous years of the First Five Year Plan,
and one first reads them as optimistic overflows of the feeling that all is
possible, an imagination rushing a few steps on from what fills every
mind or happens before all eyes.

Yet something is wrong. Chernikov's ideas are more heraldic and less
grounded in reality than those frivolous strings of garden pavilions
trying on all the styles of the past in indecent haste. Their message is
closer to 'nothing is possible', at least for architects, now that invention
and production have come completely apart.

In these early years of Stalinism some of the most wonderful
proposals, like the gigantic pictorial buildings of Melnikov, are shaped
by the sinking conviction they can never be built. Melnikov's entry in
the Palace of the Soviets competition of 1932 is more responsive to
Russian realities than Le Corbusier's, yet (like the winner Iofan's)
further from physical likelihood. The political climate was driving
architects to imagine the unfeasible and then occasionally offering to
construct it, a promise it couldn't fulfil.

For various reasons it is probably lucky that Melnikov didn't win this
competition, first of all because his idea is an effective socialist realism,

Two late projects by Konstantin Melnikov. *Above:* competition entry for the Palace of the Soviets, 1933. *Below:* project for a Commissariat of Heavy Industry, 1934.

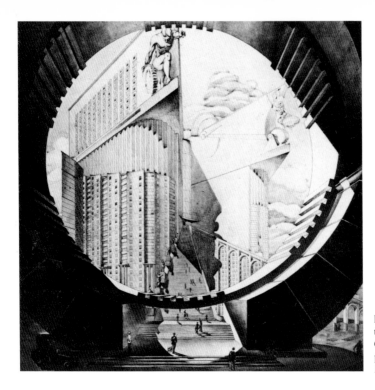

Konstantin Melnikov: portal
to an endless stair of the
Commissariat on the previous
page, a fantasy that brings
Melnikov close to Piranesi.

instead of the moribund variety which triumphed in the real world. For all its ingenuity, his project if built would have been one of the most crushing physical facts on earth. It is a conflation of two incompatible masses of ancient pedigree – a pyramid and a colosseum, like a diagram of society torn between aspiration and oppression, between down bearing masses and expansive shell-forms. The whole effect is broken, even if on the grandest scale, reality wrenched into new shapes by violence like the paradoxes of a Baroque poem.

A few years later his proposal for a Commissariat of Heavy Industry is *heavy* with a vengeance, the largest letter M in the world. Much of his energy went into gloomy Piranesian perspectives, showing endless ascents, passing through heroic cog-wheel portals to enter the building many storeys above ground. No one would ever successfully complete an errand here; it couldn't be built because there isn't time for the experience it presumes in the spectator.

One can argue the place of deliberate impossibility in architecture, buildings flooded by water their greatest enemy, or so vast they defeat the dimensions of the human frame and are untraversible. But though it may seem that Melnikov has given us such paradox here, it is instead a realistic depiction of the way the scale of modern Soviet life had temporarily made architecture impossible.

Notes

p.13 Gardens reconstructed: The recent fashion for period authenticity in gardens well surveyed in John Harvey, *Restoring Period Gardens*, Aylesbury, 1988. Concentrates on England, good on methods and continuing projects, includes useful gazetteer.

p.13 Shakespearean plants at Anne Hathaway's Cottage, Stratford-on-Avon (and in many botanical gardens in English-speaking countries), Napoleonic (mostly old roses) at Malmaison, Chateau.

p.14 Pope: line from *Epistle to Burlington*, 1731. The poet was a passionate gardener who wrote an influential essay on the subject (*The Guardian*, 1713). His own garden at Twickenham was a tourist attraction; an elaborate contemporary description is reprinted by Hunt and Willis, *The Genius of the Place*, 1975, pp.247–53. Only the grotto survives, in a denuded form.

p.15 Le Nôtre: see *Oxford Companion to Gardens*, 1986, for up-to-date account of his career and the principles of his designs. For illustrations see F. Hazlehurst, *Gardens of Illusion*, Nashville, 1980.

p.15 Eugène Atget 1857–1927, sold his photographs to artists to use as models and seems to have viewed them as documents. About 8500 survive, the bulk of them now in the Museum of Modern Art, New York. Gardens fill the third of four volumes published by the museum as *The Work of Atget*, 1983.

p.16 Bird's eye views: John Harris, *The Artist and the Country House*, 1979, contains over 400 views, covering a continuum from plan to view with many bird's eye stages in between. Primitive examples often the most suggestive, conceptually. Harris' introduction surveys early Continental analogues.

p.18 Stourhead: In *The Stourhead Landscape* (a National Trust guidebook), 1971, Kenneth

Woodbridge catalogues the surviving structures and comments on changes in the planting over centuries. He does not consider extravagant allegorical interpretations like Ronald Paulson's, who reads the garden as if it were Book VI of the *Aeneid*.

p.20 Jefferson's architecture: See F. Kimball, *Thomas Jefferson, Architect*, Boston, 1917. For Jefferson's encounters with European buildings and gardens, see the letters in *Thomas Jefferson, Writings*, Library of America, 1984.

p.20 Shobdon: One result of the transfer (in 1751–2) of these sculptural highlights to the garden is that they have weathered at an accelerated pace. Now the tympanum can be deciphered much more easily from the 19c cast in the V&A than from the original in Herefordshire. On 17c and 18c attitudes to Romanesque, see 'Rediscovery of the Romanesque' in the exhibition catalogue *English Romanesque Art 1066–1200*, Arts Council, 1984.

p.21 Hameau: The hameau documented in an album the queen ordered from C.L. Chatelet with 26 watercolour views, now in Estense Library, Modena. See *La Révolution française et l'Europe 1789–1799*, exhib. cat., Paris, 1989, no 44. Originally there were twelve buildings; nine survive. The domain was the scene of agricultural and botanical experiment, intimate meetings and lavish parties.

p.21 'Dairies' in England: A few famous primitive dairies by Soane (at Hamels in Hertfordshire, bark was left on the columns and woodbine encouraged to twine itself round them). Many illustrations and examples in J.M. Robinson, *Georgian Model Farms*, Oxford, 1983.

p.22 Capability Brown: Useful gazetteer and description of his surviving projects in Roger Turner, *Capability Brown and the eighteenth century English landscape*, 1985.

p.22 Italian grottos and underworlds: See *Oxford Companion to Gardens*, 1986, for classical roots, a wonderful early snippet from Alberti, and a rich mix of references.

p.23 Bomarzo: 25 miles S. of Orvieto. Margaretta Darnall gives a clear account of this confusing place in *Oxford Companion to Gardens*, 1986. For good pictures of each element and plans of the whole, *Vicino Orsini und der Heilige Wald von Bomarzo, ein fürst als künstler und anarchist*, by H. Bredekamp, photos by W. Janzer, 2 vols, Worms, 1985.

p.24 Wales: Meic Stephens, *Oxford Companion to the Literature of Wales*, Oxford, 1986, under Tours of Wales.

p.24 Lake District: Norman Nicholson, *The Lake District*, Harmondsworth, 1977, an anthology, and *The Discovery of the Lake District*, V&A, 1984.

p.24 Highlands: J. Holloway and L. Errington, *The Discovery of Scotland*, National Gallery of Scotland, 1978.

p.24 Victorian gardens: for good pictures, see Alastair Forsyth, *Yesterday's Gardens*, RCHM, 1983.

p.24 Mazes: Lavish illustration in H. Kern, *Labyrinthe, Erscheinungsformen und Deutungen 5000 Jahre Gegenwart eines Urbilds*, Munich, 1982.

p.24 Japanese gardens: L. Kuck, *The World of the Japanese Garden*, 1972.

p.28 Topiary: Good survey from Roman times in Jellicoe, Goode & Lancaster, *Oxford Companion to Gardens*, Oxford, 1986. Abuses of the form are normal.

p.28 Arts and Crafts gardens: Mawson, Robinson and Blomfield (the last two bitter enemies) are the main names, Mawson's illustrations to his own books are very telling.

p.30 Gimson: Five cottages, including a second home for his brother, on the edge of Charnwood Forest in Leicestershire. Old photographs show that much of the effect of the best, Stoneywell, was lost when slates replaced thatch on the roof after a fire. For Bedale's school, see M. Comino, *Gimson and the Barnsleys*, 1980, where Gimson's Hall, Library, and Chapel are fully illustrated.

p.31 Brockhampton: An extreme example of a handmade building; its story in G. Rubens, *W. R. Lethaby, Life and Work*, 1984. Randall Wells,

Lethaby's foreman on this site, built a church at Kempley, Glos, not far away.

p.31 Naturalism in Gaudi's buildings: The main examples include the dragon gate at Finca Guell, the tile roof and other details at Casa Battlo, the billowing masonry of Casa Mila, the sculpture of the Nativity façade of Sagrada Familia, and above all the crypt and its porch at the unfinished Colonia Guell chapel. All are well illustrated in C. Martinell, *Gaudi, His Life, His Theories, His Work*, (Spanish ed, 1967) Barcelona, 1975.

p.34 Villandry: Parterres by the Spanish artist Lonzano for Joachim de Carvallo (restorer of the gardens, who worked from Renaissance treatises, 1906–24). Four gardens of love in box hedge: Tragic Love (swords and daggers in red symbolizing blood spilt), Adulterous Love (horns, fans, and love letters in yellow, colour of deceit), Tender Love (hearts separated by orange flames of love, masks in centre), and Passionate Love (hearts broken in two by passion, in pattern representing dance).

p.34 Lutyens and Jekyll: For their collaboration, see Jane Brown, *Gardens of a Golden Afternoon*, 1982. Many of Gertrude Jekyll's books recently reissued by Antique Collectors' Club. Hestercombe, now Somerset Fire Brigade Headquarters, is open to the public. Great Dixter, Sussex, is another important Lutyens garden which may be visited.

p.34 Sissinghurst: Biographical interest threatens to overpower other sorts at Sissinghurst (in Kent, 2 miles NE of Cranbrook). Vita Sackville-West, its deviser, epitomizes the Bloomsbury set.

p.34 Stowe: The gardens have recently been transferred to the National Trust, which is embarking on a long programme of restoration and repair. Some strange plunderings have taken place: Robert Lorimer borrowed columns from the Temple of Concord to reuse them in a school chapel he built in the grounds.

p.36 Chiswick House garden: Considerable remnants of the gardens, well documented in a good DoE guidebook. Plans to reinstate some missing features now afoot.

p.37 Iconic features glaring down: In the last few years this has changed. Throughout the Soviet bloc, slogans (like 'All Praise to the Soviet People') and images have been coming down.

p.37 Stalin's deification: Infrequent but lavish Soviet publications on architecture from the 1930s and late 1940s are strangely monument-centred, with magnifications of the ruler (in free-standing statues, heads in relief near rooflines, clubs and cities named for him) discreetly sprinkled through the pages of mass-housing projects.

p.38 Lutyens did more than fifty war memorials in England and the colonies in the years 1919–27 and was responsible for 126 military cemeteries in France and Belgium. In these works, and of course in New Delhi, he seems truly the architect of the end of empire.

p.40 Christo's wrapped projects: *Christo–Der Reichstag*, Frankfurt, 1984; for other wrappings see *Christo*, exhib. cat. Tokyo, 1987–9.

p.40 Hitler's architectural plans: Recent publications on Albert Speer, Hitler's collaborator in these monstrous projects, have sometimes viewed his work with grotesque admiration. See, for instance, L. Krier, ed, *Albert Speer, Architecture 1932–1942*, Brussels, 1985, a mausoleum of a book.

p.41 Memorials in Washington: *The Outdoor Sculpture of Washington D.C.* by J. Goode, 1974, gives much interesting detail about the commissioning of monuments and illustrates many minor ones. H. Caemmerer, *Washington, The National Capital*, Government Printing Office, 1932, is exhaustive on government buildings up to that date.

p.41 Lincoln Memorial: An amazing early proposal in the form of ten towers (connected near the top by railways) was exhibited as a huge panoramic painting by Erastus Salisbury Field, now in Springfield (Mass) Museum of Art (exhib. cat. by Mary Black, 1985).

p.41 John Russell Pope: Three folio volumes on his work c. 1950 show some Adirondack lodges in a primitive style (à la Soane or Ledoux) along with country houses and government commissions.

p.43 Monte Grappa: 20 miles N of Bassano in the Veneto, Cima Grappa, a massive tiered mound, all of Grappa stone, with a marshal's tomb and shrine to the Virgin of the Mountain at the centre. Completed in 1935, it is the largest memorial of the Mussolini period.

p.44 On Nazi use of parades and military festival, see R. Taylor *The Word in Stone, The Role of Architecture in National Socialist Ideology*, Berkeley, 1974.

p.45 Gettysburg: The Eastern Park and Monument Association publishes a pamphlet *The Location of the Monuments, Markers and Tablets on Gettysburg Battlefield*, 1982, reprinted 1984, which is unillustrated but packed with information.

p.47 Egyptian Revival: Piranesi was first. He had studied the rich Egyptian collections in Rome and in the 1760s pioneered the use of Egyptian motifs, notably in the Caffè degli Inglesi in the Piazza di Spagna. Napoleon's campaign (in 1798–9) revived the subject in France. See N. Pevsner and S. Lang, 'Egyptian Revival', in *Studies in Art, Architecture and Design*, vol 1, 1968.

p.48 Mies's Liebknecht/Luxemburg memorial: An accidental commission. To do it cheaply he used rough over-fired bricks, which were free for the haulage.

p.49 Stockholm cemetery: *Erik Gunnar Asplund*, AJ Masters of Building, ed Dan Cruickshank, 1988, concentrates on buildings rather than landscape. For the architect with whom Asplund shared the commission, see *Sigurd Leverentz 1885–1975, The Dilemma of Classicism*, Architectural Association, 1989. Many other cemetery projects are illustrated.

p.49 Richard Long: R. Fuchs, *Richard Long*, Guggenheim Museum, New York, 1986, contains a series of mock-prehistoric monuments in mountainous landscapes all over the world.

p.50 Christo's Running Fence: Erected September and removed October, 1976, elaborately recorded in Werner Spies, *Christo: Running Fence*, New York, 1977, and C. Tompkins and D. Bourdon, *Christo: the Running Fence*, New York, 1978.

p.50 Franklin's house: *Benjamin Franklin's 'Good House'*, 1981, sold at the memorial, gives an amusing account of the search for the missing house 1950-73, after which Venturi's ghost of the building was commissioned.

p.52 House-memorials: *The Cambridge Guide to the Museums of Britain and Ireland*, with over 2000 entries, has at the back a list of 200 museums 'associated with individuals'. This includes many writers', inventors', and statesmen's houses, but also some places more arbitrarily or tangentially connected.

p.54 Obscure Provençal poets: an unfair reference to the Museon Arlaton in Arles, a rich trove of local tradition founded by the Provençal poet Frédéric Mistral.

p.54 Fascist memorials: The most interesting fascist memorial to an Italian hero never got built, Terragni's *Danteum*, planned (c. 1938) for a site near the Colosseum in Rome. It consisted of emblematic rooms representing the realms of Dante's thought: Inferno, Purgatorio, Paradiso, and – a Fascist insertion – Imperio. The influence of de Chirico's paintings of c. 1914 has been detected in these bleak and noble spaces.

p.54 Mercenaries of the Renaissance: see under *Condottieri* and names of individuals (Hawkwood, Gattamalata, Colleoni) in *The Thames and Hudson Encyclopedia of the Italian Renaissance*, ed J.R. Hale, 1981.

p.55 Stalingrad: Perhaps a book can now be written on the Soviet inspired cult of the monument in Eastern Europe, 1948–89. Separate boastful works, like a booklet on monuments in Tallinn (Estonia), 1987, already exist.

p.55 Statue of Liberty: On 30 May 1989 a statue of polystyrene and plaster, described as the Goddess of Democracy and based on the Statue of Liberty (though she held her torch with two hands), was erected by art students in Tiananmen Square, Peking. On 4 June this figure c. 25 feet high was toppled by the People's Liberation Army as it retook the square, killing thousands. Pictures in *The Independent*, London, 10 June 1989, p.30, with text of June 2nd Hunger Strike Declaration.

p.55 Statue of Liberty: In *The Statue of Liberty*, Harmondsworth, 1974, Marvin Trachtenberg, an art historian, inspired by a visit with his sons, gives the monument full dress scholarly treatment.

p.56 Oldenburg colossi: See Claes Oldenburg, *Proposals for Monuments and Buildings, 1965–69*, Chicago, 1969, which illustrates about 45 projects.

p.59 Mount Rushmore: Gutzon Borglum's first mammoth project, to Confederate heroes, at Stone Mountain, Georgia, begun 1916, foundered in controversy. Rushmore was begun in 1927 and remained incomplete at his death in 1941 (R. Dean, *Living Granite. The Story of Borglum and the Mount Rushmore Memorial*, 1949). An earlier colossus was Bartholdi's lion at Belfort (on the French/German border); latterly an enormous bust of Ferdinand Marcos, taking shape on a Philippine hill, was shown on British television around the time of his demise, 1985.

p.60 Washington Monument: See G. Olszewski, *History of the Washington Monument*, Washington, 1971, which illustrates strange alternative proposals and charts the painfully protracted construction.

p.61 Sir Walter Scott Monument: 1840–6 by G.M. Kemp, a Border shepherd's son. Competition brief specified the Gothic style. Besides the seated novelist with deerhound Maida at his side, the spire is decorated with 84 statues of his characters (see Gifford, McWilliam and Walker, *Buildings of Scotland: Edinburgh*, 1984, pp.314–6).

p.61 Palace of the Soviets: The subject of an international competition in which there were some notable entrants, among them Hans Poelzig and Le Corbusier. Melnikov's and Leonidov's the most interesting Russian proposals.

p.62 Rockefeller Center: Now sold to Mitsubishi, see recent book on Wallace K. Harrison, the chief architect.

p.62 Brancusi: His studio makes a strange exhibit in the courtyard of Pompidou Centre, Paris. For relation of the monuments to his other sculptures see Sidney Geist, *Brancusi: The Sculpture and Drawings*, New York, 1975.

p.64 Vietnam Memorial: The competition was won by a young Chinese-American. Her enigmatic work (completed 1982) provoked a counter-monument nearby, a kitschy over-lifesize bronze of two soldiers (one obviously black) supporting a wounded comrade.

p.67 Ruskin on war: in last section of *Modern Painters III* ('The Teachers of Turner'), which concludes with a rhapsody on the Crimean War.

p.67 Architecture in Wales: Serious books about Welsh buildings are beginning to multiply: J. Hilling, *The Historic Architecture of Wales*, Cardiff, 1976; various RCHM volumes, including one on vernacular houses; and two volumes (so far) of a projected six on *The Buildings of Wales*.

p.69 Michelangelo's fortifications: J. Ackerman, *The Architecture of Michelangelo*, 2 vols, 1961, devotes a chapter to the Florentine designs of 1528–9, seeing them as episodes in the history of warfare and in Michelangelo's career as a sculptor interested in problems of movement. At San Miniato, defences designed by Michelangelo were temporarily constructed of packed earth mixed with straw.

p.70 Thomas Tresham's buildings: All three near each other in central Northamptonshire. Triangular Lodge, Rushton, the smallest and most complex, in DoE care (guidebook). His unfinished crystalline house, Lyveden New Bield, administered by the National Trust (guidebook). His small market hall is in the centre of Rothwell.

p.71 Salses: Just off the N9 between Perpignan and Narbonne. The Caisse nationale des Monuments historiques, which supervises the fortress, publishes a guide with good schematic drawings of the defences.

p.72 Berkhamsted castle, Hertfordshire: was a crucial place in history of the form. Scene of Saxon surrender (see *Anglo Saxon Chronicle*) it may be first Norman castle constructed in England. See brief DoE guide, and *Castles, An Introduction to the castles of England and Wales* by B. O'Neil, HMSO, 1973, with useful set of plans.

p.72 Iron Age hill-forts: C. Hawkes, 'Hillforts', *Antiquity* 5, 1931, 60–97, and D. Harding, *Hillforts*, 1976.

p.74 Town fortifications: For Berwick, see pp.83–4 and note, Lucca's walls built 1504-1645, with eleven bastions, never used, still intact, now forming a circular tree-lined walk. Naarden, best preserved Netherlandish example of 17th-century moated embanked fortification.

p.74 Fortified houses in Scotland: N. Tranter, *The Fortified House in Scotland*, 5 vols, Edinburgh, 1962–70. Includes 600 examples each with a drawing by the author, but no plans. D. MacGibbon and T. Ross, *The Castellated and Domestic Architecture of Scotland*, 5 vols, 1887–92, had a pronounced influence on the course of Scottish architecture around the turn of the century.

p.75 Castle-prison design: Robin Evans, *The Fabrication of Virtue, English Prison Architecture 1750–1840*, Cambridge, 1982, incorporates original thinking and research.

p.75 H.H. Richardson, Buffalo asylum: see J. Ochsner, *H.H. Richardson: Complete Architectural Works*, Cambridge, Mass, 1982, 1984.

p.76 Burghley House: Soke of Peterborough, now Cambridgeshire. See N. Pevsner, *Buildings of England, Bedfordshire, etc*, Harmondsworth, 1968.

p.77 Wollaton, Hardwick, and Bolsover: All treated in M. Girouard, *Robert Smythson and the Elizabethan Country House*, New Haven, 1983 (retitled revision of 1967 ed). Girouard's guide to Hardwick and the thorough DoE one to Bolsover (with good plans) give more detail.

p.78 Burges Castles: Castell Coch, 5 miles N of Cardiff, in DoE care, who publish a good guide. Cardiff Castle, more lavish, less perfect, administered by Cardiff City Council.

p.78 Castle Drogo: 4 miles NE of Chagford (Devon), National Trust guidebook available with pictures of full size cardboard mockups of unbuilt parts which Drewe got Lutyens to make.

p.81 Lecce: see volume in *Le città nella storia d'Italia* series, by M. Fagiolo and V. Cazzato, Rome/Bari, 1984.

p.81 Fascist counter centre: An example in Pisa between the railroad station and the old core.

p.81 Tàranto, Bari: Minimal details in *Puglia*, Touring Club Italiano, Milan 1978, with architects' names and dates. A few pictures in *Bari* volume of *Le città nella storia d'Italia* by M. Petrignani and T. Porsia, Rome/Bari, 1983.

p.82 Viollet-le-Duc: In *Viollet-le-Duc*, exhib. cat., Paris, 1980, a large section on restorations, with many before-after drawings of Carcassonne's defences.

p.82 Berwick on Tweed, Northumberland: Unique in England for its well preserved Renaissance bastion defences, dating from soon after the form's invention in Italy (1558–69). An exemplary DoE guide by Iain Macivor, with good explanatory drawings.

p.85 Palmanova and Renaissance ideal cities: Rather sketchily in H. Rosenau, *The Ideal City, Its Architectural Evolution in Europe*, 1959 (new ed, 1983), interesting sources, smudgy illustrations.

p.87 Mississauga: The architectural competition recorded in *Mississauga City Hall, A Canadian Competition*, New York, 1984, ed. by P. Arnell and T. Bickford. All 246 entries are illustrated.

p.88 Pienza: A large literature in Italian, see bibliography in *Toscana*, Touring Club Italiano, Milan, 1974.

p.89 Richelieu: Lemercier was its designer. See A. Blunt, *Art and Architecture in France: 1500–1700*, Harmondsworth, 1953, 2nd ed 1970.

p.89 Chaux: Princeton Architectural Press reprinted Ramée's edition (1847) of Ledoux's *L'Architecture* in 1983. Chaux is elaborately presented there.

p.92 Shakers: Furniture and appliances in many Eastern U.S. museums, but the best place to sample their spirit is the deserted settlement a few miles S of Hancock in western Massachusetts (near NY border). See J.H. Ott, *Hancock Shaker Village, a Guidebook and History*, 1976.

p.92 Sapperton, Glos: At Pinbury and then Sapperton, Gimson and the Barnsley brothers lived a life steeped in Englishness. Accounts in Lethaby's beautiful book of 1924, *Ernest Gimson and His Work*; also in M. Comino, *Gimson and the Barnsleys*, 1980. Surviving Arts and Crafts buildings and fittings catalogued by D. Verey, *Buildings of England: Gloucestershire, The Cotswolds*, 1970, 1979.

p.93 Darmstadt: See Ian Latham, *Joseph Maria Olbrich*, 1980.

p.93 Hampstead Garden Suburb: Besides Unwin's books, see various local publications: B. Grafton Green, *HGS 1907–1977, A History*, 1977; A. Lester, *Hampstead Garden Suburb: The Care and Appreciation of its Architectural Heritage*, 1977; Shankland Cox, *Hampstead Garden Suburb Plan for Conservation*, 1971 (available at HGS Trust Office, Temple Fortune).

p.94 Parker and Unwin: See *Barry Parker and Raymond Unwin, Architects*, Architectural Association, 1980.

p.95 Portmeirion: Its inventor, Clough Williams Ellis, a master publicist who wrote a guidebook, *Portmeirion, Its What? When? Why? and How? Variously Answered*, reprinted 1983, which is naturally authoritative on his intentions.

p.96 Williamsburg: The official title is Colonial Williamsburg. Colonial Parkway passes under the historic centre in a tunnel. The *Official Guide*, 1979 ed (sold in the huge visitor centre on the outskirts), is printed on antique paper and dissects the town building by building.

p.96 Disneyland: Serious planning began in 1952, and it opened in 1955. The illusion is more complicated than most observers will grasp. R. Schickel gives interesting details and explains Walt's deep and continuing involvement in *The Disney Version, The Life Times Art and Commerce of Walt Disney*, 1968, 1986.

p.99 Clérisseau ruin-room: It was rediscovered c. 1962. A good biographical account in R. Middleton and D. Watkin, *Neoclassical and Nineteenth Century Architecture*, London and New York, 1980 (orig. Italian ed, 1977). See also *The Age of Neo-Classicism*, exhib. cat., Arts Council, 1972, for detailed description of decor, including colour scheme.

p.100 Piranesi: Particularly in four *Grotteschi* published in *Opere varie*, 1750. See J. Wilton-Ely, *Piranesi*, exhib. cat., Arts Council, 1977.

p.102 Sham-ruins: A long digression at beginning of chapter on Strawberry Hill in K. Clark, *The Gothic Revival*, 1928, 1950, 1962.

p.103 Soane's house: 13 Lincoln's Inn Fields, preserves Soane's vision with amazing fidelity. J. Summerson, *A New Description of Sir John Soane's Museum*, sold at the museum, is an exemplary guidebook.

p.105 SITE, ruined stores: See *A&V*, Extra Edition, Tokyo, 1986.

p.106 Italian earthquake village: Place in NE Campania marked *Aquilonia Vecchia* on maps (in typeface used for antiquities) is the village abandoned in 1930 after an earthquake, for a site 2km to the SW. Many of the deserted buildings, such as the old hotel, appear habitable.

p.111 Festival of Britain: M. Banham and B. Hillier, *A Tonic to the Nation. The Festival of Britain 1951*, 1976. Rousing recollections and some architectural views which make one lament its passing.

p.111 C.D. Friedrich: Many of his works now in East Germany; see H. Börsch-Supan, *Caspar David Friedrich*, Munich, 1974. His sketchbooks and drawings reproduced in *Caspar David Friedrich, Das gesamte graphische Werke*, Herrsching, n.d. (a reprint).

p.112 Geology: A. Geikie, *Founders of Geology*, 1897, 1905, tells the story of its beginnings and shows how the thinking was located in a few particular landscapes, the Auvergne, the Wye Valley, and North Wales, among others.

p.116 Bevagna: For these odd re-uses of classical fragments see *Ombrie Romane* (Zodiaque), 1980, which contains good photographs.

p.117 Palazzo Bucelli: The Montepulciano museum devotes an entire room to the activities of the collector who created the strange sculptural collage of this façade.

p.117 Etruscan funerary art: The best collections are found in Volterra, Chiusi, and Cortona, each of whose small museums is modestly remarkable.

p.118 Arles and Lucca amphitheatres: Arles: in medieval times a fortified enclave containing 200 houses and a church. Excavated 1828, when all trace of habitation removed and the elaborate central sub-structure uncovered, which to the untutored eye looks like cells for gladiators and pens for wild animals. Lucca: dwellings in the middle removed 1830-9, but others still fill the Roman structure, and form a multistorey ovoid ring. A market now held in central space.

p.122 Factory in Macclesfield Road, London EC1: In fact this building was demolished between the writing of this sentence and an attempt to photograph the site.

p.122 Industrial archaeology: so called, a recent phenomenon. The term first appears in 1950s, explosion of studies in Britain in 1970s. See bibliography in W. Minchinton, *A Guide to Industrial Archaeology Sites in Britain*, 1984, for selection of regional surveys in print and type-script. Recent issues of *IA Review* will give notion of current work (reports on RCHM textile-mill surveys in Yorkshire, Manchester and Cheshire, for example). Outside Britain: *Les Chateaux de l'Industrie*, Paris/Brussels, 1979, is a photographic survey of industrial remains in Lille region of N. France. *The Lower Merrimack River Valley, An Inventory of Historic Engineering and Industrial Sites*, North Andover, Mass, 1978, a detailed gazetteer compiled by a local museum and a Federal agency. Many works such as these show that a scientific form of nostalgia is widespread at this moment.

p.122 Pisa, Arsenal: Built in 1588 for the fitting up of gallerys of the Ordine dei Cavalieri di S. Stefano. Consists of six wide bays, all formerly opening to river. See *Toscana*, Touring Club Italiano, Milan, 1974.

p.123 Breweries: Burton on Trent is the best place to see both derelict and functioning breweries.

p.123 Ducts, walkways, etc: This is a description of the mechanism for unloading coal which used to fill the space between Battersea Power Station and the river. See note to p.127.

p.124 British hi-tech: Its two leading exponents, Rogers and Foster (formerly partners) in D. Sudjic, *Norman Foster, Richard Rogers, James Stirling: New Directions in British Architecture*, 1986. Nicholas Grimshaw, a later arrival, now the subject of lavish publications.

p.124 Lloyds of London building: This contro-versial, much publicized work explained by Rogers in *Richard Rogers Partnership, Lloyds of London*, Edizioni Techno, 1986.

p.127 Battersea Power Station: built 1929-35. First of London power stations to which Sir Giles Gilbert Scott gave an impressive architectural dressing. He was called in when it was already under construction. Closed in 1983, the building is now being turned into a theme park, entailing much defacement of the fabric and its meaning. See B. Cherry and N. Pevsner, *Buildings of England: London 2: South*, 1983: and G. Fisher and G. Stamp, *Catalogue of the Drawings Collection of the RIBA: The Scott Family*, Amersham, 1981 (interesting comparison with Scott's church designs of the same years).

p.127 Warehouses of Shoreditch: Well illustrated in *South Shoreditch, Historic and Industrial Build-ings*, a Hackney Society Report, 1986. A gazetteer street by street and a plea for conservation of these buildings.

p.127 Isle of Dogs: Now the biggest building site in Europe and a catalogue of architectural horrors. The development has prompted a spate of publications, much of it bumpf to spur invest-ment, but also *London Docklands, Heritage Trail– Isle of Dogs*, LDDC, 1985, research by E. Sargent, LDDC Conservation Officer, many of its recom-mended highlights since demolished. *Outline History of the Isle of Dogs*, Island History Trust, 1987, is told from the inhabitants' point of view. The next volume of the Survey of London will treat this area (old Borough of Poplar). A Docklands museum was opened by the LDDC a few years ago but very soon closed, with no reopening projected.

p.129 D-Day harbours and Apollo launch sites: Both illustrated, along with fascinating range of industrial dereliction, in R. Steinberg, *Dead Tech*,

A Guide to the Archaeology of Tomorrow, San Francisco, 1982.

p.131–160 Locations of paintings:
Byzantine Madonnas – National Gallery of Art, Washington
Pinacoteca, Siena
S. Maria dei Servi, Siena (by Coppo di Marcovaldo)
Lindisfarne Gospel – British Library, London
Pomposa refectory, 50 km. N of Ravenna, in Po delta
Giovanni di Paolo, *Birth of John the Baptist* – National Gallery, London
Pollaiuolo, *St Sebastian* – National Gallery, London
Campin, *Madonna by fireside* – National Gallery, London
Joseph with mousetraps – Cloisters, New York
Piero della Francesca, *Flagellation* – Ducal Palace, Urbino (stolen in 1975 and recovered a year later)
Uccello, *Hunt* – Ashmolean Museum, Oxford
Pontormo, *Joseph* panels – National Gallery, London
Stanley Spencer – works in Tate Gallery, London,
Sandham Memorial Chapel, Burghclere, Hampshire
Caron, *Augustus and the Sybil* – Louvre, Paris
Clovio, *Farnese Hours* – Pierpont Morgan Library, New York
Patenier, *St Jerome in a Rocky Landscape* – National Gallery, London
Mantegna, *Dido* – National Gallery of Canada, Ottawa
Crivelli, the series of works in National Gallery, London
Elizabethan portraits:
Marcus Gheeraerts the Younger *Thomas Lee* – Tate Gallery
Ditchley portrait of Elizabeth I – National Portrait Gallery, London
Gower, *Elizabeth I* – Woburn Abbey
Flemish, *Connoisseurs in a Cabinet* – National Gallery, London
Elsheimer, *Minerva* – Fitzwilliam Museum, Cambridge
Lotto, *Andrea Odoni* – Hampton Court Palace
Gerrit Dou, *Poulterer's Shop* – National Gallery, London
Vermeer, series of works in Rijksmuseum, Amsterdam
Anon, *Edward VI at His Father's Deathbed* –

National Portrait Gallery, London
Hogarth, 'limerick mentality' – the series in Soane Museum and Tate Gallery, London
El Greco, *Moneychangers* – numerous examples including National Gallery, London
Gethsemane – Museum of Art, Toledo, Ohio
Bruegel – all works referred to are in Kunsthistorisches Museum, Vienna
C. Fabritius, *View of Delft* – National Gallery, London
Degas, *Woman seen through doorway* (Lemoisne 438) – private collection, USA
Woman at Window – Courtauld Institute, London
Vicomte Lepic and daughters (Lemoisne 368) – presumed destroyed in war

p.141 Antoine Caron: See the exhibition catalogue *L'École de Fontainebleau*, Paris, 1972, which includes six paintings, ten drawings, and two doubtful works by this scarce painter.

p.142 Clovio: Friend of Bruegel who collaborated with him occasionally. His *Farnese Hours* on which Vasari says the painter spent nine years, published in facsimile, 1976. A memorable portrait of Clovio by El Greco (Naples, Capodimonte) shows him holding this book.

p.144 Elizabethan portraits: For a somewhat strangely ordered selection of these images, R. Strong, *The English Icon: Elizabethan and Jacobean Portraiture*, 1969. The best places to see them, apart from various country houses, are Tate Gallery, National Portrait Gallery, and Ranger's House, Blackheath.

p.146 Connoisseur's cabinets: Some painstaking reconstructions of dispersed examples and unravelling of their density in O. Impey and A. MacGregor, eds, *The Origins of Museums, The Cabinet of Curiosities in Sixteenth- and Seventeenth-Century Europe*, Oxford, 1985. Paintings of these early museums in S. Speth-Holterhoff, *Les Peintres flamands de Cabinets d'Amateurs au XVII siècle*, Brussels, 1957; and O. Millar, *Zoffany and His Tribuna*, 1966.

p.159 Architecture inspired by grain elevators: The most powerful expression of this point of view in Le Corbusier, *Vers une architecture*, 1923 (in English, *Towards a New Architecture*, 1927).

p.160 Mondrian's early work: Best seen at the Hague Gemeentemuseum, catalogued by Cor Blok, *Piet Mondriaan* (a spelling Mondrian dropped c. 1911) *Ein catalogus van zijn werk in Nederlands openbaar bezit*, Amsterdam, 1974.

p.160 Mies van der Rohe's Barcelona pavilion: Built as German national pavilion for International Exhibition of 1929 and demolished when the exhibition closed, has recently been reconstructed in the original rich materials.

p.161 Friedrich Gilly: Many of his most interesting drawings destroyed in the war. See *Friedrich Gilly 1772-1800 und die Privatgesellschaft junger Architekten*, exhib. cat., Berlin Museum, 1984, which illustrates many picturesque works as well as the better known, apparently classical ones.

p.162 *Hypnerotomachia Polifili*, by Francesco Colonna, 1499: An eccentric architectural fiction. The illustrations, seen in isolation, have come to stand for a certain combination of cool restraint and mysterious oddity, as if they concealed some cultic meaning.

p.162 Kafka sketches: Surprisingly often Kafka's parables turn on spatial conundrums, which might be seen as raw materials for architecture: Franz Kafka, *Parables and Paradoxes*, bilingual ed, New York, 1961.

p.163 Michael Graves sketches: Sheets of small comic sketches tumbling over a single sheet abound in *Michael Graves, Buildings and Projects 1966–1981*, New York, 1982.

p.164 Boullée: Good brief biography with list of executed and unexecuted works in R. Middleton and D. Watkin, *Neoclassical and Nineteenth Century Architecture*, London and New York, 1980. Good illustrations in H. Rosenau, *Boullée and Visionary Architecture*, 1976 (includes his *Essai sur l'art*).

p.164 Monument to Newton: The romantic tomb for Newton a popular subject in Revolutionary France, proposals by P-J Delespine and J-N Sobre. In 1800 the Institut de France proposed a competition on the theme.

p.166 Unbuilt domes: Lutyens' design for Liverpool cathedral, his most Michelangelesque. A model made in 1933 (over ten feet high and sixteen feet long) now in Walker Art Gallery, Liverpool. The crypt was built and survives under Gibberd's cathedral; see *Lutyens*, Hayward Gallery, 1981. Speer, Volkshall terminating the N-S axis of the reshaped Berlin (South Station at the other end). Leon Krier's disturbing book (see note

to p.40) analyzes this solemnly, imagining a spectator's progress toward it. Speer wanted a masonry dome, but Hitler opted for steel and glass.

p.166 Wren's early designs for St Paul's: The rejected proposals collected in Wren Society vol I, 1924. Vol XV, 1938, includes photographs taken from *inside* the Great Model.

p.166 Wren's Great Model: shown in crypt of St Paul's.

p.167 Buckminster Fuller domes: *The Artifacts of R. Buckminster Fuller, A Comprehensive Collection of his Designs and Drawings*, ed J. Ward, 1985. Vols 3 and 4, *The Geodesic Revolution*, treat Fuller's ideas as far from a joke and derive the domes from a mapping exercise; thus they represent the world in a fairly direct way.

p.167 Telford bridge: See *The Engineers*, exhib. cat., Architectural Association, 1982, where a series of bridge designs is treated.

p.168 Finsterlin: Brief treatments with some illustration in D. Sharp, *Modern Architecture and Expressionism*, 1966, and W. Pehnt, *Expressionist Architecture*, 1973 (trans from German).

p.170 Erich Mendelsohn: He followed the three-stage model of a career detailed on p.168. Fully treated in B. Zevi, *Erich Mendelsohn: opera completa–architetture e immagine architettoniche*, 1970 (and in reduced version, English paperback, 1985).

p.170 Hat factory: 1921–23 at Luckenwalde, the next important commission after the Einstein Tower. Department store: 1926–28 at Stuttgart, for Schocken. Many of his important buildings in this decade are large retail establishments.

p.172 B. Goff: Oklahoma has the greatest concentration of Goff works, which are by and large not found near the sophisticated East and West coasts. The new Japanese gallery in Los Angeles an exception. See D. De Long, *Bruce Goff, Toward Absolute Architecture*. Cambridge, Mass, 1988, which represents a kind of canonization of this ultimate maverick.

p.173 Lequeu: In *Lequeu, An Architectural Enigma*, 1986, Philippe Duboy plays a Duchampian game regarding his theories about Duchamp's fakery. The 'works' are well reproduced by Duboy, and readers may decide.

p.174 Revolutionary Russia: For all the arts in this period, see D. Elliott, *New Worlds, Russian Art and Society 1900–1937*, 1986, which suppresses Stalinist excesses less than modern Soviet works, which are more lavish and more partial. For architecture: A. Kopp, *Town and Revolution, Soviet Architecture and Urbanism in the Twenties*, 1967.

p.175 Tatlin: His memorial to the Third International, a mammoth tilted tower, was carried round the streets of Leningrad between 1920 and 1926 in the form of a fifteen-foot model. *Tatlin*, ed L. Zhadova (Hungarian ed, 1984), 1988, contains rich illustrative material, much of which is new.

p.175 Ladovsky: led the extreme anti-formalist faction at Vkhutemas when Leonidov was a student (c. 1927) which only shows how topsy turvy ideological labels can be.

p.175 Chernikov: His *Architectural Fantasies*, 101 of them, in colour, reproduced in special issue of *Process: Architecture*, 26, Tokyo, 1981, along with unsuccessful attempts to fill in the missing biography.

p.176 Konstantin Melnikov: The most interesting architect of the period can be followed in S.F. Starr's *Melnikov, Solo Architect in a Mass Society*, Princeton, 1978, from modernist to fantast to heroic 'realist'.

Photographic Acknowledgments

(*a*: above *b*: below *l*: left *r*: right)

By gracious permission of Her Majesty the Queen
149: Aerofilms Ltd 85; Amsterdam: Rijksmuseum
151; Berlin: Staatliche Schlösser und Gärten 113;
Burton upon Trent: Bass Museum 123; Photo
courtesy Calmann and King Ltd, London 158;
Cambridge: Fitzwilliam Museum 101 *a*, 148,
University of Cambridge, Committee for Aerial
Photography 73; Peter Chèze-Brown 75, 84 *r*;
Christo and C.V.J. Corporation/photo Wolfgang
Volz 40; Jeremy Cooper Ltd 31; Country Life 63 *l*;
© 1985 Walt Disney Productions 96; English
Heritage 36; Florence, Casa Buonarroti 69 *r*; Grania
Forbes-Robertson 39 *l*; Ewing Galloway 41; General
Electricity Authority 127; Gettysburg National
Military Park – U.S. National Park Service 47;
Giraudon 21; Michael Graves 163 *r*; Collection
Captain Loel Guinness, on loan to Tate Gallery,
London 144; The Hague: Gemeentemuseum 159;
Courtesy of the Hampstead Garden Suburb
Archives Trust 94; Brian Hatton 117, 118; Intourist
Moscow Ltd 55; Collection Carroll Janis 57, 58;
Japan Information Centre, London 26; Susan Jellicoe
27; Ed Jones and Michael Kirkland/photo courtesy
Building Design 87; A.F. Kersting 33, 68, 71, 77, 80,
83; Emily Lane 84 *l*; Lloyd's of London/photo Janet
Gill 125; London: Architectural Association (photo
Edith Caldecott) 32 *b*, (photo Hugh Dutton) 49;
(photo Bill Forrest) 126, (photo A. Higgott) 39 *r*,
(photo Marjorie Morrison) 15, (photo Site Inc) 105,
British Library 133 *r*, British Museum 168, National
Gallery 135, 136 *l* & *r*, 139, 147, 150, 155 *a*, 157,
National Portrait Gallery 145, 153, Port of London
Authority Collection, Museum in Docklands 128,
Sir John Soane's Museum 101 *b*, 104 *l* & *r*, 167 *b*, St
Paul's Cathedral Library 167 *a*, Tate Gallery 140;
Hamish MacInnes 115; Mansell/Anderson 134; Bil-
darchiv Foto Marburg 43; Mas, Barcelona 32 *a*;
Montreal Museum of Fine Arts 920.104 143 *r*; New
York: Collection, The Museum of Modern Art. The
Abbey-Levy Collection. Partial gift of Shirley C.
Burden 17 *a* & *b*, Pierpont Morgan Library M 69 143
l; Oxford: Ashmolean Museum 138; Paris: Biblioth-
èque Nationale 165 *a* & *b*, 173, Louvre/Photo
Réunion des Musées Nationaux 141; Alain Perceval
72; Private Collection, Switzerland, courtesy,
Anthony d'Offay Gallery, London 50; Royal Com-
mission on the Historical Monuments of England 79;
Running Fence Corporation 1976/photo Jeanne-
Claude 51; Siena: S. Maria dei Servi 133 *l*; Collection
Sirot, Paris 56; Edwin Smith 18, 23, 35 *b*, 60, 95, 103,
114, 120; Photo courtesy of South Dakota Depart-
ment of Tourism 59; Stockholm: Royal Swedish
Academy 19; Dr Franz Stoedtner 171 *r*; Stuttgart:
Staatsgalerie 169 *a*; Taunton: Somerset Fire Brigade
35 *a*; Tîrgu Jiu Public Park, Romania (Photo
Sheorghe Serban) 62, 64; Toledo Museum of Art,
Gift of Edward Drummond Libbey 155 *b*; Urbino:
Galleria Nazionale delle Marche 137; Venturi,
Rauch and Scott Brown/photo Mark Cohn 52;
Vienna: Kunsthistorisches Museum 156 *a* & *b*;
Washington Convention and Visitors Association
65; Winterthur: Courtesy, the Henry Francis du
Pont Winterthur Museum 93; Zurich: Kunsthaus
109.

Index